My Senior Moments Have Gone High-Tech

Karen O'Connor

HARVEST HOUSE PUBLISHERS
EUGENE, OREGON

Cover by Dugan Design Group, Bloomington, MN

Author photo © Michael Pettrey Photography, michaelpettreyphotography.com

Published in association with Books & Such Management, 52 Mission Circle, Suite 122, PMB 170, Santa Rosa, CA 95409-5370, www.booksandsuch.com.

MY SENIOR MOMENTS HAVE GONE HIGH-TECH
Copyright © 2016 Karen O'Connor
Published by Harvest House Publishers
Eugene, Oregon 97402
www.harvesthousepublishers.com

Library of Congress Cataloging-in-Publication Data
   O'Connor, Karen.
   My senior moments have gone high-tech / Karen O'Connor.
      pages cm
   ISBN 978-0-7369-6510-1 (pbk.)
   ISBN 978-0-7369-6511-8 (eBook)
   1. Older Christians—Religious life. 2. Aging—Religious aspects—Christianity. I. Title.
   BV4580.O375 2015
   248.8'5—dc23

                                           2014021859

Printed in the United States of America

15 16 17 18 19 20 21 22 23 24 / BP-JH / 10 9 8 7 6 5 4 3 2 1

For all my senior friends.

Acknowledgments

My thanks to each of these men and women who contributed suggestions and ideas and their own experiences, which I used with their permission as "story seeds" for this book:

Pat Baer • Dianne Barker • Jennifer Butenschoen • Peggy Dickerson • Charles Flowers • Heidi Heath Garwood • Donna Goodrich • Jim Gordon • Janet Kobobel Grant • Linda Gail Johnson • Rose Kabat • Jade Kinnaman • Jennifer Zarifeh Major • Diana Brand Meyer • Brenda Nixon • Charise Olson • Yvonne Ortega • Bonnie Rose • Columba Lisa Smith • Laura Strnad • Jeremy Sturm • Julie Sweeney • Georgia Varozza • Sandra Victor

Contents

Tech Bloopers

1. Time of Day. 13

2. Can't Trust 'Em These Days 15

3. Mouse Hunt 17

4. Stubborn Critter 20

5. One Is Enough 22

6. M[o]usings 24

7. Mind Scan. 26

8. Anything Goes. 28

9. How Dare You! 30

10. Rear Window 32

11. Whack Whack. 34

    Fun Quiz #1. 36

Computer Blunders

12. How Generous! 39

13. All in a Name. 41

14. Eek! A Mouse in the House!. 43

15. No Talking Back 45

16. Computer Dating 47

17. Back Up. 50

18. Surfin' the 'Net 52

19. Fandango. 54

20. Right or Right Left? 56

21. A Fax Fix 58

22. Bye-Bye Files 60

23. It's Right Here! 62

24. Pedal, Pedal 64

25. Power Play 66

26. Are You There? 68

27. Locked Out 70

28. Yahoo for the Google! 72

29. Computer Lodge 74

30. Right or Left? 76

    Fun Quiz #2 78

Email Mishaps

31. Lasting Impression. 81

32. Email Canada Style 83

33. Yellow Pages. 85

34. Creative Spelling 88

35. Email Shemail 91

36. Sorry About That. 93

37. A Bunch of Characters. 95

38. Gee! Mail! 97

39. Email Bail 99

40. I've Got Mail 101

    Fun Quiz #3 103

Smartphone Foibles

41. India Jones 107

42. Charge! 109

43. Upgrade Upset 111

44. Outside Her Comfort Zone 113

45. Pay as You Go—or No! 115

46. Out in the Cold 117

47. I Just Don't Get It 119

48. You Call This Customer Service? 122

49. Flippin' Funny 124

50. Setting Things Straight 126

51. Wrong Number 128

52. Chatty Cathy 130

53. Lights, Camera, Action! 132

54. Cellitis 134

Social Media Meddlings

55. "Friending" the Friendless 139

56. Something New 141

57. Net [Not] Working 143

58. Fierce Competition 145

59. Facing Facebook 147

    Fun Quiz #4 149

Harebrained Hardware

60. iBad 153

61. All Keyed Up 155

62. All Gone 157

63. Fan Club 159

64. Run for Cover 161

65. Kick the Kindle 163

66. Decisions...Decisions! 165

67. Frozen Tundra 167

Password Paranoia

68. One Key at a Time 171

69. Star-Studded Password 173

70. I Pass 175

71. Pick a Password 177

Tech Support Troubles

72. Pretty Cool 181

73. Got It Covered 183

    Fun Quiz #5 185

I lift up my eyes to the mountains—
where does my help come from?
*My help comes from the L*ORD*,*
the Maker of heaven and earth.
Psalm 121:1-2

Tech Bloopers

1

Time of Day

Mickey and her housemate, Ginny, headed for the Sierra Mountains, both ready for a few days off. They set up their tents in the campground at Lake Dorothy. No motor home for them. They preferred camping the old-fashioned way. They took a daily hike on the well-marked trails and returned in the late afternoon to prepare dinner on their camp stove. In the evening, they sat around the fire pit with the stars twinkling overhead in the dark sky.

It was a great time of exercise and relaxation. On the first day, before setting off on their hike, Mickey suggested they turn off their cell phones. "Our cells are right here," she said, patting her backpack. "To be used for emergency only."

Ginny agreed.

At the end of the week, the women packed up Mickey's car and drove down the highway toward home. They'd been out of touch with the outside world for several days and had no idea what was going on in their city or around the globe. A few hours later they pulled into a truck stop for drinks and a sandwich. Mickey felt the urge to check on things, so when they piled into the van again she suggested Ginny turn on the radio. "We ought to be able to get some news and music now."

Ginny worked the knobs on the radio. "What frequency?" she asked.

"Try 102.3—our favorite country music station."

After fiddling with the dials for a long time, Ginny sat back and sighed. "I give up. I can get 1-0-2, but 1-0-2 point 3 won't come in. I don't understand what's going on. It's always worked before.

Mickey glanced over at the radio and noticed it was turned off. The *clock*, on the other hand, indicated 1:02.

The women giggled so hard, Mickey had to pull off the road until she and Ginny could compose themselves enough to continue driving safely. They'd definitely been out of touch too long.

TECH TIP

Put on your glasses, if necessary, when reading maps, radio station numbers, and cell phones—if you don't want to get lost.

Reflection

His God instructs him and teaches him
the right way (Isaiah 28:26).

Contemplation

"It's supposed to be automatic, but actually
you have to push this button."

JOHN BRUNNER

Timely Prayer

When it comes down to it, Lord, people are pretty funny creatures, needing your help even with the simplest of things.

2

Can't Trust 'Em These Days

"My grandma Marion is adorable when it comes to new technology," said Charlotte. "She uses Whiteout Liquid Paper on the TV remote to mark the important buttons. She once went weeks without watching television because she'd inadvertently pushed the wrong button. She had to wait for someone to come over to help her."

Marion also has her doubts about modern washing machines. She isn't sure hers *really* cleans the clothes, so she soaks them in the washer tub, stirs them with a stick, and then she lets the machine run its cycles.

As for the dishwasher, she uses it for storage only because she doesn't believe it can clean her dishes as well as hand washing.

One year for her grandmother's birthday, Charlotte made an appointment with her daughter Mandy, who was away at college, to attend the celebration via a Skype phone call. "It took a little doing because there isn't Internet access at Grandma's house," said Charlotte, "and I'm not very tech-oriented either. But I was so excited to have Grandma see and talk to Mandy during the party that family members and I managed to get it all set up. When it came time to talk with Mandy, Grandma sat in front of the screen straight as a stick. She barely talked, and she only did so or waved when one of us prompted her. It was strange."

The call lasted only a few minutes, and Charlotte admits she was a little disappointed. "Later I asked Grandma why she was so reluctant to participate. Turns out she thought it was a *video*. She believed we were putting on a skit for her as we interacted with Mandy. She couldn't believe it was a live call or that was really Mandy speaking directly to her.

TECH TIP

Do a run-through explaining what's happening before using new technology with reluctant seniors.

Reflection

In all your ways submit to [the LORD],
and he will make your paths straight (Proverbs 3:6).

Contemplation

"I have always wished for a computer that would be
as easy to use as my telephone. My wish came true.
I no longer know how to use my telephone."

BJARNE STRONSTRUP

Timely Prayer

Lord, I'm so excited when a new possibility comes along,
but so often the old way seems easier.

3

Mouse Hunt

Laurene was going to learn to use a computer if it killed her—and it almost did! She tried to follow the suggestions her son gave her when he sat down with her, but he talked so fast and moved so quickly typing this and searching for that, that she couldn't keep up with him. He also used a little silver box attached to the computer to move from one place to another. He called it a "mouse" of all things. It didn't look like a mouse to her.

One day Laurene took matters into her own hands. She called a local computer store and asked about tutoring. The gentleman on the line told her they offered a class for seniors on Tuesday mornings from ten o'clock until noon. There were two spots left. "Ma'am, if you'd like one of them, it's yours."

Laurene signed up. She felt quite proud of herself. She didn't tell her best friend or her son her plans. She would learn what to do and then surprise everyone with her expertise—as soon as she became an expert, that is.

The following Tuesday morning, Laurene showed up at "Click! Click! Computers" and found a seat in the last row. She was a nervous wreck. Her palms perspired and her stomach jittered. She didn't want to make a fool of herself.

The facilitator was a nice young fellow with dark hair and a warm smile. He introduced himself as Jeremy and then explained some of the basics. Later he walked from table to table, looking over the shoulder of each person as he or she practiced. Jeremy helped where it was needed and offered suggestions when he observed a problem.

Then he issued a short assignment. "Use the mouse to locate Google in the upper-right-hand corner of your browser—Firefox. "Touch the mouse, and you'll see a blinking line. That's called a 'cursor.' It's your starting point when you're about to click on something or type. So let's all do this together. Using the left button on your mouse, click on Google. Now there's a box in the middle of your screen, and your cursor should be blinking inside it. Type in the words 'movie theaters' and then press the 'Enter' key on your computer. What came up?"

Several people raised their hands. "A list of movie houses in our community," called out one man.

"I got the same thing," said another. Most people nodded in agreement.

Laurene broke out in a sweat. She didn't get that. In fact, she didn't get anything. The mouse slid all over the screen. She saw the little box with the word "Google," but when she put the mouse right on top of it nothing happened.

Suddenly Jeremy was at her side. "Are you having trouble?"

"Yes. My mouse isn't working. Maybe it needs a new battery."

"Show me what you did, and then I can help you."

Picking up the wireless mouse, she placed it on the monitor. "See? Nothing."

Jeremy shielded his mouth.

Was he about to laugh at her? Laurene was certain she'd turned ten shades of red.

"Ma'am, here's your problem." Jeremey gently removed the mouse from her hand and placed it on a pad next to the computer. This is called a 'mouse pad.' You work the mouse from here, not on the screen."

Laurene was humiliated, but she smiled and said, "Thank you." She decided she had a long way to go before she could brag to her son and best friend that she was a computer expert. She grabbed the mouse and moved it on the pad until the cursor landed on the Google search box. She clicked the left button. From there she could catch up with the others in her class.

TECH TIP

You *can* tame a computer mouse.

Reflection

God is...an ever-present help in trouble (Psalm 46:1).

Contemplation

"The problem with troubleshooting
is that trouble shoots back."

AUTHOR UNKNOWN

Timely Prayer

Thank you, dear Lord, for technology. Help me keep it in perspective though. It will never be more powerful than prayer.

4

Stubborn Critter

Eric kept a basket on the coffee table in the den for all manner of gadgets—TV remote, wireless mouse for his laptop, cell phone, cordless home phone, a screwdriver, extra batteries, and even a candy bar or two.

One evening when his wife was at her book club, Eric settled down in front of the television to watch a couple of police procedurals, the kind of shows Cindy wanted no part of. He set himself up with a bowl of popcorn and an ice-cold root beer. (Cindy didn't approve of that either.) He fished the TV remote from the basket and clicked. Nothing. Not a spark of light or a bit of sound. "Rats! Not again!" he mumbled. "Why can't technology ever work? Those techie geniuses make more than their share of the fortunes in this world. You'd think they could create a television that would turn on without having to petition Congress first!" He opened the remote and changed the battery to be on the safe side. He clicked and clicked. Still no response. He finally grabbed a magazine and crawled into bed. TV would have to wait for another day.

A couple of hours later, Eric heard Cindy's key turn in the lock on the front door. He was happy to know she'd arrived home safely. When she slipped into bed beside him, he told her his woeful story about the obstinate TV remote. "It's times like this when I wished we had two TVs," he said. "I missed a whole evening of my favorite shows because of that gadget."

Cindy listened, but she didn't understand why Eric had struggled. She'd watched a show that very afternoon, and the remote had been as responsive as ever.

The following morning, Cindy asked Eric to bring her the remote.

He brought it to the kitchen where she was dishing up scrambled eggs. She looked up and suddenly let out a belly laugh. "Eric, this is the *computer* mouse, not the TV remote. Have you forgotten what the TV remote looks like or what?"

Eric took a look at the item in his hand and hung his head. "This getting old is getting the best of me," he said. He gave her a hug. "It seems I can't do anything without you these days."

"Does that mean you're stuck with me?" Cindy said, giggling.

"No, it means we're sticking together."

Cindy planted a kiss on Eric's cheek. "I like the sound of that."

TECH TIP

Take a close look at the gadget you pick up and make sure it's the right one. Saves a lot of time and headache.

Reflection

When I am afraid, I put my trust in you (Psalm 56:3).

Contemplation

"I'm naming my TV remote Waldo."

AUTHOR UNKNOWN

Timely Prayer

Blessed am I, Lord, because when I misuse or misplace a gadget, you help me figure it out or find it.

5

One Is Enough

Roger called tech support. He was at his wit's end with his antiquated computer. He knew he should probably spring for a new one, but at his age was it worth it? What if he ordered it today, it was delivered next week, and he died the following day? All that money down the drain.

"You can't look at life like that," said his sister Maddie. "Live as though you have all the time in the world. Spend your money. Enjoy yourself. Stay up-to-date."

Maddie sounded convincing. He'd call tech support this time and then plan an outing next week to find a new computer that fit his budget.

Someone from tech support responded to Roger's call.

"Sir, I can help you with that. It's a simple fix. Just follow my instructions. I'll be here to support you."

"Sounds good to me," Roger said. "I'm a little flummoxed at the moment. I can't see as well as I used to."

"No problem. I'll stay on the line until you're completely satisfied that I've answered all your questions and you get to where you want to go on the Internet."

Roger breathed a sigh of relief and then listened carefully. He was almost finished when the tech man threw him a curve.

"Okay, now click your left mouse button."

Roger panicked. "What? My left mouse button?"

"Yes, sir."

"Oh! I'm so embarrassed. I didn't know I was supposed to have a left and a right mouse. I only have the one. What should I do now?"

TECH TIP

You can click left or right on the same mouse.

Reflection

Reflect on what I am saying, for the Lord
will give you insight into all this (2 Timothy 2:7).

Contemplation

"Disappointments were not meant to destroy you.
They were meant to strengthen you and give you
fortitude to accomplish your God-given talent."

KEMMY NOLA

Timely Prayer

I'm praising you, God, for being at my side no matter
what situation I find myself in and for always providing
a way out when I need one.

6

M[o]usings

Jake bought his mom a laptop, but she frowned at the sight of it. "What do I need a computer for?" Donalda asked.

"Mom, you're only 72. Think about how it will change your world—open it up and give you more access to your friends and family. You'll love it, I promise."

Donalda wasn't so sure she wanted her world to change. She liked it just the way it was. She had her sewing circle on Mondays, line dancing on Wednesdays, and church with the family on Sundays. That was enough activity for one week!

But Jake wouldn't take no for an answer. He was certain his mother would appreciate the gift once she got the hang of it. So he talked her into enrolling in a computer class to receive the basic training and support necessary to be successful. In fact, he offered to attend the class with her.

Donalda agreed—reluctantly—as long as her son joined her. On the first day of class, the instructor welcomed the students and then gave a PowerPoint presentation to illustrate the basics. Following that, he strolled around the room, going from desk to desk checking each student, answering questions, and making sure they were all on the same page.

He stopped at Donalda's desk. She'd placed the mouse on the floor and rested her right foot on top of it. The coach bent down, asked her to move her foot, and then picked up the device. "The mouse belongs on the desk next to your computer," he said. "Like this." He placed the object within reach of her right hand.

Donalda covered her mouth with a hand and giggled. She looked around, hoping Jake, who was sitting in the back row, hadn't seen what happened.

"Move the mouse with your right hand," the instructor continued as he demonstrated how it worked.

"Oh my," said Donalda. "I thought it was for my foot—you know, like a sewing machine." She looked around again and then leaned toward the man. "Please don't tell my son. He's sitting in the back row."

"Don't worry," he said and patted her hand. "It will be our little secret."

TECH TIP

Keep your hand on your mouse so it won't get away.

Reflection

[The Lord said,] "I will lead the blind by ways they have not known, along unfamiliar paths I will guide them" (Isaiah 42:16).

Contemplation

"Just because something doesn't do what you planned it to do doesn't mean it's useless."

THOMAS EDISON

Timely Prayer

Good thing you're with me always, dear Lord—even in a computer class—or I'd be sunk.

7

Mind Scan

Lee agreed to be "on call" over the weekend. It might mean running all over town to fix people's tech problems, but, on the other hand, maybe no one would need help and he'd have a few days off but still get paid. Pretty good deal as far as he was concerned.

The office phone rang, and Lee picked up the call, hoping for a quick fix without having to make an in-person appointment.

"My scanner hasn't worked for two weeks. Why haven't you fixed it yet?" The customer was obviously irate, and his voice escalated the longer he talked.

Lee looked through the customer tickets file online, but there was no one listed by the name of the caller. "Have you called in before? Did you place a service order? If so, did someone give you a ticket number?"

"I don't know what you're talking about. What is this about a ticket? Sounds as if you're running a raffle instead of a Customer Service Department for people like me. I gave you my hard-earned money for a simple piece of equipment...only to find out the thing doesn't even work right."

"Well, fortunately, I have an open appointment today. I can drop by about noon and take a look. I'm sure we can get it back up and running in no time."

Close to noon, Lee drove up to the customer's house. He got out and knocked on the door. When the man answered, they talked briefly and Lee was invited in. Lee followed him into the room with the scanner. He took a look at the machine, and it seemed to be perfectly fine.

"See? Absolutely no response when you push the buttons. What do you have to say about that?" The customer folded his arms across his chest and pursed his lips in disgust.

Lee turned to the customer with a smile. "How long has it been unplugged?"

TECH TIP

It's a good idea to check all connections before calling a technician. Saves time and avoids a red face.

Reflection

Be patient and stand firm (James 5:8).

Contemplation

"Technology...is a queer thing.
It brings you great gifts with one hand,
and it stabs you in the back with the other."

C.P. SNOW

Timely Prayer

Oh dear! Too often I blame the other guy instead of paying attention to my part in a debacle. Thank you, God, for redeeming my ignorance.

8

Anything Goes

"Buzz, this is Mom. Sorry to bother you at work, but I'm in a pickle again. Some of this computer stuff is beyond me—or maybe I just need new glasses." She sighed because she hated to appear ignorant to her son.

"It's okay, Mom. Better to ask a question than to be stuck all day without your email and Internet. I know you like to shop online too. What can I help you with?"

"It's that 'any' key. I can't find it on the keyboard. Why do the manu-facturers make everything so complicated? Don't they realize that older folks need things to be simple and large enough so we can see what we're doing?"

"Mom, slow down," Buzz said, letting out a breath.

"You sound upset with me."

"Not at all, but you're talking so fast, I can't get a word in. I want to help. Tell me what's going on."

Lolly sat down and sighed again. "I'm online ordering a book, and a message came up after I filled out my info that says, 'Press any key to continue.' I cannot find the 'any' key for the life of me. Now what do I do?"

Buzz chuckled.

"Now don't you make fun of me. I'm your mother, you know. And I didn't grow up with computers like you did."

"Mom, relax. I'm not making fun of you. Whenever there's a pause in a buying process, the system is telling you to press *any keyboard but-ton* to continue."

"There isn't a specific 'any' key?"

"You're right, there isn't one. The instructions are telling you to choose *any* key you want: k, j, w, e—you pick one, press it, and your order will go through to the next step."

Lolly knew her face was turning red. She was happy Buzz couldn't see her. "Thanks, Son. You're the best."

TECH TIP

Don't panic when something seems confusing. Reread the instructions carefully and the answer should be revealed. If you remain stuck, ask for help.

Reflection

The Lord lifts up those who are bowed down (Psalm 146:8).

Contemplation

"The only way to make sense out of change is
to plunge into it, move with it, and join the dance."
ALAN WATTS

Timely Prayer

Thank you, dear Lord, for the gift of other people who know more than I do and who are willing to help when I'm in need.

9

How Dare You!

"Marie, take a look at this. It's outrageous! And to think we spent our hard-earned retirement money to purchase this piece of junk."

Harold's wife walked into the den and was surprised to see her husband's face as red as a Christmas-tree bulb. "What's all the fuss about?"

Harold pointed to the screen. "Read it. Some jerk sent me a message from who knows where and called me an 'invalid.' Not only that, the person also told me I was 'bad.' What's next? I'm going to report this to customer service. How insulting. Maybe our computer has been hacked. That must be it."

Marie put a hand to her mouth. Being the techie in the house, she knew exactly what was going on, and the situation was perfectly normal. She faced Harold. "Honey, there is nothing to worry about. What you're seeing is an error message. You put in an old disk, and apparently it's been corrupted. B-A-D is referring to the disk, not you."

Marie tackled the next dilemma. "The error message that says 'Invalid' isn't referring to your physical condition. It means that some step in your order or process is *in-valid*, meaning something isn't working. There could be a problem with the program that doesn't have anything to do with you. We'll check it out with Ben when he comes for dinner. Grandkids can fix anything. Just relax until he gets here." She kissed Harold on the forehead and then poured him a cold glass of orange juice.

He reached for her hand and kissed it. "What would I do without you?"

Marie rolled her eyes and grinned. "I can't even imagine!"

TECH TIP

Don't take error messages personally. They're generated automatically when something goes wrong with the computer or a computer program.

Reflection

You who answer prayer, to you
all people will come (Psalm 65:2).

Contemplation

"No man succeeds without a good woman behind him."

GODFREY WINN

Timely Prayer

Thank you, Lord, for people who are willing to help when I'm about to hit bottom.

10

Rear Window

Marty worked in the tech department of Olson Accounting Services. He picked up a call from the Marketing Department. It was Linda on the second floor.

"Marty, I'm having trouble with my printer. I'm not sure how to solve it."

Marty paused and then asked, "Are you running it under Windows?"

"No, my desk is near the door to Mr. Barney's office. But you make a good point. I should have thought of that. Rick's desk is under the window that looks out on the rear parking lot, and his printer seems to be working just fine. Maybe I'll see if I can move my printer next to his."

Marty took a second to control his laughter. "Linda, on second thought, it might be best if I run up and take a look. I have a couple of ideas that might work. It'll save you the hassle of moving the printer, at least."

"Thanks. You're a peach."

TECH TIP

Save yourself unnecessary work that might make things worse. Ask for help when you need it. Also, periodically review computer and software terminology so you have a better understanding of what's going on.

Reflection

The Lord preserves those who are true to him (Psalm 31:23).

Contemplation

"Once you replace negative thoughts with positive ones,
you'll start having positive results."

WILLIE NELSON

Timely Prayer

Lord, I thank you that you will help me turn a negative
into a positive when I turn to you.

Whack Whack

Bob worked in the tech department of a large catalog company. He received a call from one of the new employees—Daniel, an elderly gentleman—who was still learning the ropes.

"Will you please help me find a file on the network?"

"No problem. Click on your start button and then type whack whack, then the server name, and then the share site name. So it's 'whack whack server wack public drive.' Hit 'Enter.' That should do it."

Daniel tried several times without success. "It's not working. I'm feeling stupid and getting frustrated."

Bob suddenly realized what might be happening. "Daniel, when I said type 'whack whack,' did you spell the words out?"

"Yes. Isn't that right?"

"Not exactly. 'Whack' refers to the backslash key. How about if I come right down to help you out? It can be a bit tricky."

"Sure! That would be great."

Bob hustled to Daniel's department but made sure he wiped the grin off his face before getting to Daniel's desk.

TECH TIP

Learn the lingo, and you'll have greater success on the Internet.

Reflection

The Lord is…a stronghold in times of trouble (Psalm 9:9).

Contemplation

"Progress is impossible without change."
George Bernard Shaw

Timely Prayer

I praise you, dear Lord, for the things you do in me and
for me.

Fun Quiz #1

Circle the correct answer.

1. *Facebook*
   - bestselling book
   - social networking service
   - board game

2. *Google*
   - sound babies make
   - Internet search engine
   - brain-teaser

3. *Twitter*
   - social media website
   - first-date feeling
   - bird call

4. *WWW*
   - World Wide Web
   - Wendy's Wonder Wax
   - Win West Walk

5. *Blog*
   - drop of thick liquid
   - webpage for personal writing
   - shapeless object

6. *Firefox*
   - brand of taco sauce
   - Internet browser
   - rare mammal

Computer Blunders

12

How Generous!

Kate smiled to herself. She was catching on after a few months of playing around on the Internet. She knew how to use Google to research a topic of interest. She understood what it meant to download a file when she wanted to read a report or an article. She even started making credit-card payments online instead of writing checks. Actions that had been foreign to her just months before were becoming second nature.

Then came the day when the roof fell in, and Kate panicked. She was online and responded to a plea for a donation to a charity whose work she believed in. She had a choice—mailing a check or donating online with her credit card. *Hmmm? What should I do?* Writing a check took time and also required filling out a form, finding a stamp for the envelope, and dropping it off at the nearest mailbox. Too much work! She decided to experiment with an online donation. How hard could it be? Just a few clicks on the charity's website, and her money would be on its way. And she'd receive a confirmation by email within seconds.

Kate typed in the address of the charity. Bingo! She was now on the website. She clicked on "Donate Here" and filled out the information. So far so easy. This was fun. Kate felt sure of herself—tooling around the site without a hitch. She filled in the amount of money she planned to give and clicked "Submit."

The confirmation appeared and Kate gasped when she read, "Thank you for your $10,000 donation." *Oh no!* She'd planned to give $100! What a difference a typo could make.

It took a month to straighten out the mistake, which included a lecture of sorts from the charity's phone representative, herself a senior, about the downsides of using the Internet. She told Kate she was from the old school, which was good because she would have to fix the problem manually. And she did.

Since then, Kate hasn't made donations online.

TECH TIP

Take your time when filling out information on the Internet. It is a quick, easy, and safe way to pay bills or donate to charities as long as you double-check the "fill-ins" before clicking "Submit."

Reflection

The LORD is my light and my salvation—
whom shall I fear? (Psalm 27:1).

Contemplation

"Never trust a computer you can't throw out a window."
STEVE WOZNIAK

Timely Prayer

Lord, please be my heavenly computer guide, reminding me what to do, what not to do, and what to double-check. I don't want to be scared—just safe and sane.

13

All in a Name

Rosemary and Annette had been best friends since grade school. Now in their later years, they were separated by distance. Rosemary lived on the East Coast, and Annette moved to a retirement community near her daughter, Sarah, in Ohio. Travel was a burden for the two at their age, so they each bought a smartphone and learned to text. Both had experienced hearing loss and found it difficult to talk and hear on phones.

Sarah helped set up her mom's preferences and showed her how to use a few shortcuts when texting. Annette resisted. After all she'd been an English teacher for forty years. She didn't appreciate the newfangled way of communicating by shortening words and using abbreviations. And how confusing some of the shortcuts were! "R" for "are" and "2" for "to." "LOL" could mean "little old lady," or "lots of love," or "laughing out loud," or even "living on Lipitor"! And how about "BFF"? "Best friends forever" or, more to the point at her age, "best friend's funeral." Definitely not funny.

And then there was the auto-correct feature. One didn't even have to think these days, let alone know how to spell. Just tap a couple of keys, and the phone did your spelling for you. That was about the last straw for Annette, and she knew Rosemary would agree. Annette was careful to check her texts for errors before hitting "Send." That is, until the day when she was in a particular hurry.

Rosemary had sent a message about her son getting a new job. Then she asked Annette about Sarah and her recent medical problem. Annette fumbled with texting as she walked from one room to another, trying to do two things at once—respond to Rosemary's text and find her glasses. She hurried her response to Rosemary, texting, "Sarah is doing much better and has returned to work."

At least that's what she *thought* she'd typed. When Rosemary responded to her text, Annette saw that auto-correct had messed up her message.

"Satan?" Rosemary had texted back.

Annette burst out laughing. Auto-correct had inserted the name "Satan" instead of "Sarah." So much for a phone that was supposed to be "smart." Annette knew her daughter would get a kick out of the error too.

TECH TIP

Check your texts *before* sending. Auto-correct can cause quite a stir if it guesses incorrectly which word you wanted to use.

Reflection

Let us hold unswervingly to the hope we profess, for he who promised is faithful (Hebrews 10:23).

Contemplation

"All this modern technology just makes people try to do everything at once."

BILL WATTERSON

Timely Prayer

Lord, help me to take all these tech quirks with a smile. We are, after all, imperfect—and so are the things we build.

Eek! A Mouse in the House!

After years of working on an outdated computer, Ella decided it was time to spring for a new one. She took the brave step, knowing it would probably take some doing to get acquainted with all the changes that had occurred since her last purchase. But she was ready.

As she unpacked the beautiful laptop from its box, her heart pounded. The machine was slick and smooth to the touch and lightweight. No more heavy modem or clunky monitor. She opened it up and simply started typing. How exciting!

Ella's granddaughter was in the next room. Suddenly Lucy appeared at the door of her grandma's den. Her eyes lit up at the sight of the brand-new computer and wireless mouse.

"Grandma!" she exclaimed. "You have a new *mouse*!"

With that, Ella's husband, Nick, roared into the room with a broom. "Where? Where?" he shouted as he frantically looked around. "I'll take care of it!"

Lucy grabbed her grandfather's arm. "Stop, Grandpa! It's a *computer* mouse, not a house mouse."

"Doesn't matter what kind it is. I'll get it!" he replied heroically.

Ella and Lucy broke out laughing.

Ella held up the defenseless, plastic-covered pointing device.

Nick set down the broom and chimed in to their laughter.

TECH TIP

The computer mouse is as quiet as a...well...as a mouse.

Reflection

Their hearts are secure, they will have no fear; in the end they will look in triumph on their foes (Psalm 112:8).

Contemplation

"The ultimate promise of technology is to make us master of a world that we command by the push of a button."

VOLKER GRASSMUCK

Timely Prayer

Dear God, I'm so grateful you are at my side when I'm learning something new. Nothing is too difficult when I'm walking with you.

15

No Talking Back

Lorraine got fed up with the hand-me-down computer from a relative. She was tired of it talking back to her! She gave up on it, so her daughter Mindy bought her a new one. She suggested her mom have fun playing around with the new device.

"You can't hurt it, and you can't ruin it, Mom. So enjoy experimenting. Sometimes you learn more that way than you would in a computer class. You can go at your own pace."

A week or so later, Lorraine called Mindy. "Something went wrong," she said. "My computer was frozen. I kept pressing buttons, but nothing worked even though you said I couldn't break it. Then all of a sudden the machine started talking to me. Really!"

Mindy was quiet for a moment. "Mom, are you sure you're feeling all right?"

"Of course I'm all right!" her mother barked. "It's the computer that's all messed up. Whoever heard of such a thing? A talking computer."

"What did it say?" Mindy asked.

"Not (pause) my (pause) fault. (pause). Not (pause) my (pause) fault."

"Really?"

"Yes, really. I turned it off and got it started again, and it hasn't talked back to me since."

"Good. It sounds like you took charge, Mom. Great to hear!"

TECH TIP

If you don't want your computer to talk back to you, don't install TalkBack or any program like it.

Reflection

"Don't be afraid," the prophet answered. "Those who are with us are more than those who are with them" (2 Kings 6:16).

Contemplation

"Modern technology
Owes ecology
An apology."

ALAN M. EDDISON

Timely Prayer

Lord, I'm grateful I don't need a computer program to talk to you.

16

Computer Dating

Celeste took a few computer classes to help her feel comfortable with her new laptop. There was a lot to learn, and she knew that at her age time was running out so she'd better make the most of the opportunity while it was here.

Ramon, the young man who tutored her, was as nice and patient as one could be. He never insinuated that Celeste was too old for a computer, or slow to learn, or asked too many questions that had obvious answers. He treated her with respect and was always encouraging.

"If I were younger or he was older and available," she told her neighbor Sheila, "he'd be a great catch." The two widows giggled like schoolgirls.

"And if all that were true," Sheila added, "I'd hope he'd have a brother for me."

Celeste thought about Ramon every time she opened her computer. She looked forward to her lesson day each week—even more than her book club or weekly tennis game.

I've been alone too long she told herself. *Get a grip. He's a kid, and you're an old lady.* Such scolding didn't do any good, though. Celeste enjoyed thinking about Ramon, even though she understood they were student and teacher and nothing more. In three weeks their relationship would come to an end, and Celeste would be on her own with her computer. But at least she could return for an hour of tutoring here and there as needed. Ramon had assured her of that. Of course, there would be a fee, but Celeste would gladly pay it.

On the last day of her private lessons, she opened her laptop to check email before meeting Ramon at the computer store. There on the screen appeared a request for a date! But there was no signature or other details. Celeste was suddenly jittery all over. *Who would be so bold?* She smiled. It was kind of exciting to think about. However, she knew it could be dangerous to accept dates with strangers. She ignored the request and signed off.

Later that day she sat down with Ramon for her final tutoring session. Her imagination soared. What if Ramon was the silent suitor? Would he really want to take her out—even if just for coffee? That couldn't be. After all, she was old enough to be his mother. She put the idea out of her mind and opened her laptop. There was the message again.

She pointed to it with some reluctance. "Ramon, do you know anything about this?" she asked coyly.

"Yes, I do," said Ramon. "Apple is asking your permission to *update* all your programs so everything will run smoothly now that bugs and glitches in the existing versions have been addressed and removed. Click here and the update will occur automatically."

Celeste was certain her face turned as red as a real apple. She clicked the link as Ramon told her to do. *So much for fantasies. Back to reality,* she thought. She was an old woman trying to learn the ups and downs of computers, and he was a young man teaching her how to do that. Nothing more. Time for a *mental* update.

TECH TIP

Avoid taking risks online. Be sure you know to whom you're responding before accepting any offers. Always know the sender before opening any email. It could be a virus from a stranger. If you don't know the sender or the subject line seems strange, delete it immediately.

Reflection

I will listen to what God the LORD says; he promises peace to his people, his faithful servants—but let them not turn to folly (Psalm 85:8).

Contemplation

"It seems a long time since the morning mail
could be called correspondence."

JACQUES BARZUN

Timely Prayer

Lord, I'm happy to know that even when I mix up my
words you still get my meaning and intent.

17

Back Up

Lydia fussed and fumed at her computer. It had been a struggle to tame the beast from day one. Maybe she was just too old for this tech stuff. What was wrong with postal mail anyway? All you had to do was write out a check for a bill or compose a note or letter, put it in an envelope, affix a stamp, and drop it into a mailbox. Done. Nothing more to handle. But on a computer she had to deal with bugs and backups, sign-ins and spam. She didn't understand what this all meant, but she'd been willing to learn—up to a point. Then one day she'd just had it.

A warning message came up on her screen reminding her to "save" what she'd written before signing out and to back up all open documents to avoid losing them. *Oh my.* Now she was shaken. She felt as if the police were after her. What next? A command to put her hands up or get down on her knees?

She searched for the business card for the computer repair store not far from her home. With shaking hands she punched in the number and waited for someone to answer. Hopefully someone could rescue her.

"Computer care. How may I help you?"

"I hope you can help me," Lydia said. She couldn't control her shaking voice.

"What happened, ma'am? You sound scared."

"I am. I'm reading a message on my computer screen. It's telling me to 'Back up.' I stood up right then and backed up a good two feet. I haven't moved. What should I do next? There are no more instructions."

"Ma'am, how about if I come right over and help you out?"

"Oh, would you?"

"Of course. Give me your address, please. I remember you live near our store. Oh, and ma'am, it's okay to sit down again."

"Are you sure?"

"Yes. You can trust me on this one."

TECH TIP

When in doubt about something tech-related, better to ask for help than to take things on that you don't understand.

Reflection

Do not let your hearts be troubled and
do not be afraid (John 14:27).

Contemplation

"Everybody gets so much information all day long
that they lose their common sense."

GERTRUDE STEIN

Timely Prayer

Thank you, Lord, for providing people who know what they're doing to help me when I don't.

18

Surfin' the 'Net

Brad popped in on his grandfather Ed one afternoon after school. "What's up, Gramps? Thought I'd drop by and spend a little time with you."

Ed sat up from his easy chair and rubbed his eyes. "You caught me napping," he admitted. "I'm known to snooze a bit at my age."

"No problem. Go ahead and finish your rest. I'll just go in the den and do a little surfin'." He pulled his laptop out of his backpack.

Ed scratched his head. "Surfing? In the den? I thought you did that at the beach. Or are you talking about looking at a surfing movie?"

Brad laughed. "I meant surfing the 'net," he explained.

"Sounds like you're planning a fishing trip. What kind of net do you use? Why not stick to a good, old-fashioned pole and bait. I like…"

Brad groaned under his breath. Gramps was at it again. Get him started on fishing, and there was no telling when he'd be finished.

"Actually, Gramps, I'm talking about looking around on the *Internet*. You know, visiting a few websites. It's called surfin'—kind of like channel hopping on TV."

Ed sighed. "What will you young people think of next? Okay, I get it. You go ahead and surf the net and I'll channel hop."

With that, Gramps settled back in his easy chair and fell asleep while Brad did a little surfin'.

TECH TIP

Did you know you can find all manner of information and products by doing a little web surfin' yourself? Just type the topic into the search box on Google and an array of places to visit will pop up. Better yet, ask one of your grandchildren to surf with you.

Reflection

[LORD,] your word is a lamp for my feet,
a light on my path (Psalm 119:105).

Contemplation

"Life is a lot like surfing…When you get caught in
the impact zone, you've got to just get back up.
Because you never know what may be over the next wave."

BETHANY HAMILTON

Timely Prayer

Lord, thank you that in every situation—serious or humorous—you are with me.

19

Fandango

Cora took a deep breath before entering the computer store. She was about to deal with the irritating device she'd had for a long time. It kept freezing up on her. She'd called her daughter Patsy whenever it happened, and she'd receive the same advice every time:

> Mom, shut down your computer. Let it cool for a moment
> and then reboot. I think it's time to purchase a new one.
> You've had enough trouble with this one. It's old. Give in
> and let it retire.

Cora wasn't going to purchase a new machine. She had better things to do with her money than make the rich guys richer. She'd read somewhere that total revenue for computers and video games in the United States alone was in the bazillions. On the other hand, this freezing thing was really bugging her. She'd sit down, bring in her email, start to type a reply, and boom, the cursor locked and she couldn't go any further. She decided to take matters into her own hands. She realized her solution was probably a little unconventional.

"I'm here to buy a fan," Cora said to the young sales assistant.

"What kind of fan?"

Cora looked at her as if she had two heads.

"A fan for where I plug in my modem."

"I'm not sure I know what you mean." The woman frowned and then smiled. "Did you bring your computer with you? I'd like to take a look at what you're referring to."

"It's in my car. Can someone carry it in for me?"

"Sure. I'll be happy to."

They went out to the car, and the assistant took a look at the computer. "I see you've duct-taped a blow-dryer to the side of your machine. How does that work for you?"

"Not well at all. The computer still freezes even when I put the dryer on high."

TECH TIP

If you have a problem with your computer freezing up, take it to a technician. A hair dryer won't do the trick.

Reflection

Though he may stumble, he will not fall, for the Lord upholds him with his hand (Psalm 37:24).

Contemplation

"The greatest task before civilization at present is
to make machines what they ought to be,
the slaves, instead of the masters of men."

HAVELOCK ELLIS

Timely Prayer

Lord, when I find myself in a sea of trouble, I know you'll keep my head above water. Thank you.

20

Right or Right Left?

Tech representative Dave was about to pull out his hair. It seemed he got all the loonies. *Why do people purchase computers if they don't want to learn to use them? There's all kinds of help online for anyone with half a brain.* He chugged a can of soda, wiped his face with a cold cloth, and sat down again at the phone bank, ready for the next customer. He hoped it would be a person with some measure of intelligence.

"Hello. Dave in tech support," he said. "How may I assist you?"

"Hi, Dave. I hope you can help me. My name is Sam as in Samsung—you know the Samsung phone and TV? Ha, ha."

Oh, boy! Here we go. A comedian yet. Dave groaned quietly.

Sam explained his dilemma and then paused.

"I can help you with that," said Dave. "Here's what I'd like you to do."

He proceeded to give Sam, "as in Samsung," instructions as clearly and carefully as he could. "Please *right* mouse click *once*—only once. When you right mouse click on 'ReadyGo,' you'll get a drop-down menu. From this menu, *left* mouse click *once*—only once—on the choice that says 'Preferences.' It will be the last one on the list."

"I can't do that—sorry." Sam sounded adamant.

"What do you mean you can't do that?" Dave asked, letting out a breath to the side and hoping the customer couldn't hear his exasperation.

"I can't right mouse click because my mouse doesn't have a right button."

"You have a PC, right? Not a Mac?"

"Yes."

"All right then. The mouse you're working with has two buttons, correct?"

"Yes, but they're both left."

"Sir, they can't both be left. If you have two, one of them has to be on the right."

"I'm telling you my mouse has two buttons and they are both on the left. What don't you understand about that? Should I send you a picture? I thought you were supposed to be helping me."

"Sir, please calm down. I am here to help you. Okay, I believe you. You only have two left buttons. Just click on the *right* left mouse button."

TECH TIP

Oh my! Sometimes the customer has to help the technician...or so it seems at first.

Reflection

We have confidence before God, and receive from him anything we ask, because we keep his commands (1 John 3:22).

Contemplation

"Technology gives us power, but it does not and cannot tell us how to use that power."

JONATHAN SACHS

Timely Prayer

Lord, I feel so grateful that in you and with you I can find perfect peace—especially when I feel overwhelmed.

21

A Fax Fix

"My fax is in a fix," joked Ralph, an elderly gentleman facing a support person at a local tech store. "I'm sorry to say this, but it seems this fax machine is a piece of junk. What can you do about it? Fix it? Return my money? Repair it?"

"I'm sorry for your trouble," said Jon, the customer service rep. "I'll certainly look into this for you. And if the problem is at our end, we'll make good on it, I assure you. Please tell me exactly what is going on so I'll know what to report to our repairman."

"How am I supposed to know? Isn't that your area of expertise? I wouldn't be here if I knew what was wrong and how to fix it."

"I understand, but still it would be helpful to know what steps you've taken so far to send faxes."

Ralph clenched his jaw before relaxing it enough to say, "I made a copy of an article I wanted to send to my sister, stuck it into the opening at the bottom of the machine, and hit 'Send.' Then I waited and waited. Nothing happened." He pulled out a folded paper from his shirt pocket. Here it is!"

"I see the problem. The slot at the bottom is where the document you've just put through the fax comes out. To send it you feed it into the feeder up here at the top. Then you type in the fax number of where to send it. After that you press 'Send.'

"Well, why didn't the person who sold it to me explain that in the first place? Look at all the time we both wasted and all the gas it took to drive here."

"With all due respect, there's an illustrated guide in the instructions booklet that shows and explains each step."

"Who reads printed instructions anymore?"

"Precisely." The rep smiled and pushed the fax machine toward the owner. "I believe you're all set now. Have a nice day."

TECH TIP

Even though it's a pain, reading the instructions before using any new electronic device is worthwhile. It will save you time, and frustration, and a trip to the store.

Reflection

The testing of your faith produces perseverance (James 1:3).

Contemplation

"It does not matter how slowly you go
as long as you do not stop."

CONFUCIUS

Timely Prayer

Lord, I tend to let my impatience get the best of me. Please help me to stop, breathe, and pray for guidance before jumping to conclusions.

22

Bye-Bye Files

"Chris, this is *so* frustrating! I'm about to toss this computer out the window and go back to pen and paper. That method worked for centuries."

"Grams, it's okay. I'm sure there's a simple answer. Let's start from the beginning. You went to your computer after breakfast to check your email as you always do, right?"

"Yes. But the email seems stuck. Nothing's popping into my inbox like it usually does. Yesterday it worked fine, but this morning...well, forget it."

"Think for a minute, Grams. Did you do anything different yesterday before shutting down for the day?"

"As a matter of fact, yes. I saw on TV...or the Internet...that a person should always delete emails she doesn't recognize so you won't accidentally open one and get a virus."

"That's a good practice. Is that what you did?"

"Well, yes. I remember seeing some junk about winning money and one about buying insurance. Stuff like that."

"So you deleted them?"

"Yes. And now I can't bring up the good stuff. What should I do?"

"I'll be right over, Grams. I don't understand why this happened."

Chris rushed to her grandmother's apartment. The moment she looked at the desktop, she realized what went wrong. "Grams, you threw away the entire email program and then shut down, so I'm afraid all your emails are gone."

"No! I can't believe that happened. Are you sure?"

"Yep. See, your email icon is no longer showing on your desktop."

"Now what?"

"I can reinstall it, and you'll be fine from now on. You just won't have any of the emails you saved within the program."

Grams lowered her head.

"Remember, Grams, you can delete one message at a time if you don't want it or it scares you. But don't throw out the baby with the bath water." Chris smiled and got busy with the installation. Then she invited Grams out for coffee. Her poor grandmother could probably use a break from all this tech stuff.

TECH TIP

Periodically check your files and clean them up. "If in doubt, don't throw it out" is an excellent motto for computer use.

Reflection

The LORD your God is with you (Zephaniah 3:17).

Contemplation

"The only true wisdom is in knowing
you know nothing."

SOCRATES

Timely Prayer

Only you, dear God, know everything. Thank you for giving me the help I need when I need it.

23

It's Right Here!

Roberta had tried everything she could think of to make things right, but nothing worked. All she wanted to do was print a couple of recipes for her neighbor. But the computer message when she tried to print continued to read "Can't find printer."

She turned the computer screen so it faced the printer. Surely that would help. How could the computer not "see" what was right in front of it? Crazy! Roberta was about to pick up the printer and toss it out the window—but it was too heavy to move.

She called her son Skip and explained the situation.

"Mom, you probably don't have the correct drivers installed. I'll come over after work and solve it for you, okay? It's an old printer and a fairly new computer, so they need to be made compatible. No biggie. You'll be printing before the night is over."

Roberta threw kisses into the phone. Then she danced her way to the kitchen to prepare Skip's favorite pie as a big thank you.

TECH TIP

Sometimes the solution is closer than we think.

Reflection

[Jesus said,] "My Father will give you whatever you ask in my name" (John 16:23).

Contemplation

"Working together is success."

Henry Ford

Timely Prayer

Thank you, God, for the gift of people who are willing to share their talents and understanding.

24

Pedal, Pedal

"Mark, I hate to bother you again. But you're such a genius when it comes to computers, I couldn't resist."

"Reenie, cut that out. You know you could learn this stuff if you put a little time in. Computers today just aren't that tough to use. In fact, it's difficult to mess up if you use a little common sense."

Reenie shrunk like a peony in the rain. Her brother could be so harsh. All she needed was a little help getting started with her new computer. She made her case in a soft voice. "Please, Mark. I want to get to my email and suddenly my computer won't work."

She could hear Mark sighing on the other end of the phone. "Okay. What happens when you push the power button?"

"I thought I was supposed to use the mouse to get to my email."

"You are, but if the computer isn't powering up, the mouse won't help."

"How dumb of me. I thought if I pumped it a bit, it would wake up."

"What do you mean 'pumped it'? I don't understand."

"Like in the car. The mouse looks like a pedal, so I thought…"

"You mean you've been *stepping* on the mouse?"

"Yes. Did I miss something?"

"You did, but don't worry. And for Pete's sake don't cry. I'll be over after work."

"I knew you were a genius. I knew it."

Mark blew out a long breath, said goodbye, and hung up.

TECH TIP

Avoid experimenting. Carefully read the instructions that come with your tech equipment before using it. If you can boot up your computer and get on the Internet, go to www.YouTube.com and type in "using a mouse" for an instructional video.

Reflection

*We have confidence before God and receive
from him anything we ask* (1 John 3:22).

Contemplation

"Be not afraid of going slowly,
be afraid only of standing still."

CHINESE PROVERB

Timely Prayer

Lord, please help me carry on regardless of my age or my concerns about my ability. I know you are always with me.

25

Power Play

Gilda unpacked her brand-new laptop and set it on her desk. She was so excited to have such a lightweight machine that was so easy to put almost anywhere. No more large monitor that swallowed up her workspace. Now, if she could just get it to respond, she'd be all set. She flipped it open and waited. Then waited some more. Nothing happened. She checked the cord to be sure it was plugged into the computer and the wall socket. Yes, both were in place.

After another hour of waiting and staring at the black screen, she called customer support, ready to chew out the person who was unlucky enough to handle her call. She considered canceling payment and taking the whole kit and caboodle back to the store—or better yet demanding that someone come by and pick it up.

While she was on hold, she lamented selling her old computer. She should have waited until she was sure the new one worked.

Finally it was her turn to talk to a support representative.

"What happened when you pressed the power switch?" the young man asked.

"What power switch?" Gilda asked.

"The one in the upper right corner of the laptop base," he said.

"Oh, *that* one." Gilda tried to play it cool. She pressed the power button, and suddenly the screen lit up. "It worked. The computer turned on."

"Sounds good," the tech rep said. "It's doing its job. Thanks for calling, and have a nice day."

TECH TIP

It helps not only to plug the cord into the wall and into the computer, but to also to press the power switch.

Reflection

[Jesus said,] "I will do whatever you ask in my name, so that the Father may be gloried in the Son" (John 14:13).

Contemplation

"Life is all about learning. Learning about the little things. Learning from all your mistakes."

SUZIE PIERCE

Timely Prayer

Thank you, Lord, for continuing to teach me what I need to know in each phase of life.

26

Are You There?

Wendy logged on to the college website. She was taking a course in literature over the Internet and got stuck trying to locate some necessary information for one of her assignments. She opened the chat text box to reach the library assistant.

An answer box appeared, and the person introduced himself as Steve. He asked how he could assist her.

Wendy typed in her request.

"Please give me a second or two while I locate a couple of websites that will be useful for you."

Wendy posted "Okay" at her end. She waited and waited, busying herself with a few details on her desk until Steve got back to her. She checked her watch and thought about what she'd prepare for dinner. Then she wondered what was taking Steve so long. Finally, she glanced at the chat box and noticed there were the two responses Steve had promised. Then he'd typed, "Is there anything else I can do for you?"

Wendy was so embarrassed. She was glad Steve couldn't see her face. She wondered how long *he'd waited for her* to acknowledge him and sign off.

"I must have been daydreaming," she said later, "because the help I needed was right in front of me. I just wasn't tracking. My mind had gone on autopilot. I quickly thanked him and signed off while wondering if he thought I was some ditzy college student who couldn't keep it together. On the other hand, maybe he'd be right."

TECH TIP

If you have a question or comment, a chat box, if offered, is a great way to reach someone quickly. Note where it's located and check it frequently for a response to your query.

Reflection

The LORD will be my light (Micah 7:8).

Contemplation

"We need two kinds of acquaintances, one to complain to, while to the others we boast."

LOGAN PEARSALL SMITH

Timely Prayer

Dear God, thank you for giving me the ability to learn, dream, and plan. Help me keep on track.

27

Locked Out

Annie was so annoyed she was about to pull her hair out—the little she had left. "The program isn't working correctly!" she said to her work partner, Ginger. "It keeps locking up."

"Sounds like it's been a bummer of a morning for you. I understand. I've had days like that too."

"I hate my computer. I never had this problem thirty years ago when I started working."

Ginger brightened. "Hey, Annie, I think I know what the problem is!"

"Great! I can use all the help available."

"Round up your purse, your sweater, and your car keys."

Annie looked at Ginger as though she'd lost her mind. "What are you talking about?"

"Just one more step, and you'll be all set. Shut down your computer and..."

Annie interrupted. "If you're going to tell me to reboot and restart the program, I've already done that."

"No, not that. Something that will be truly helpful. Now, stand up, push your chair back under your desk, and go down to the parking garage. Start your car and drive home. Come back tomorrow and..."

"Are you nuts? I can't just walk out!"

"Okay, at least take a bathroom break. When you return, I'll help get you up and running."

Annie broke out laughing but took Ginger up on her suggestion to take a break and relax. The rest of the day ran smoothly.

TECH TIP

When having tech trouble, stop, look, listen, and try again. If that doesn't work, take a break to clear your mind and release frustration.

Reflection

You, LORD, keep my lamp burning (Psalm 18:28).

Contemplation

"Since we cannot change reality, let us change
the eyes with which we see reality."

NIKOS KAZANTZAKIS

Timely Prayer

God, here I am again, needing your grace and guidance. Thank you for putting people in my life who understand and can help.

28

Yahoo for the Google!

Fred bought himself a laptop for his eightieth birthday and was thrilled with the lightweight machine. He couldn't travel anymore due to arthritis pain and just plain old age, so his computer would be his ticket to the world outside the little village of Hillside, where he'd lived most of his life.

He also looked forward to learning more about subjects that fascinated him, such as American history and exotic animals. He might even do some poking around for info about his ancestry. Someone told him all he had to do was "Google" a topic by typing it into the Google search engine. A list of websites to visit would supposedly pop up. Click on one or more of those, and he could get more facts than he'd ever imagined or hoped for.

Googling soon became Fred's daily hobby, and he got quite proficient with his searches. He attended a basic computer class at the store where he purchased his laptop, and that helped too.

Eventually Fred noticed that he was losing interest in getting together with his friends because most of the old duffs weren't interested in growing and expanding their knowledge base. They were content with reruns on TV or kibitzing about the government over coffee at the local diner. That wasn't for him anymore. He'd found a way to stay current, learn more about the past, and challenge his mind to keep expanding.

He even opened an email account with Yahoo. He was having fun in his old age and wasn't about to quit. His new response when people asked how he was doing became his motto. "Yahoo for the Google!"

he'd shout. And if they scratched their heads wondering what he was talking about...well, he'd just smile and keep on going.

TECH TIP

If you want to use your time wisely and learn more about the subjects that interest you, make friends with Google, Yahoo, and other search engines.

Reflection

The house of the righteous contains great treasure (Proverbs 15:6).

Contemplation

"Always bear in mind that your resolution to succeed is more important than any one thing."

ABRAHAM LINCOLN

Timely Prayer

Thank you, Lord, for the gift of knowledge and the ability to learn and grow no matter how old I get.

29

Computer Lodge

Marvin taught a computer class for seniors in order to earn a little extra money while getting his computer science degree. One morning while setting up the class, an elderly student strode to the front of the room.

"How do I lodge in to Wahoo email?" he asked.

"I think you mean *log* in, not *lodge* in. And the email program is *Yahoo*, not *Wahoo*. First you need to type in your username and password in the fields that request them and then hit 'enter.'"

"I don't have either one."

"Okay. That just means you don't yet have an account. I can help you set that up."

"I don't need your help for such a simple thing. I just want to know what to do. I'll have you know I have a PhD! I was teaching physics before you were born."

"All right then, I'll leave you to it." Marvin turned back to his notes.

"Well, I guess I could use a little help. I'm not a computer genius like you are."

Marvin heard some sarcasm in his tone and wondered where it was coming from.

"By the way, I want to *lodge in*, not *log in*. Pretty funny that *I'm* teaching *you* the proper vocabulary."

"The correct term is 'log in.' You can't log in without a username and password."

"Look, I don't care about all the fine print," the student insisted. "I just want to pick up my email. Several of my friends have tried to send me messages, and they're wondering why their emails are bouncing back."

"You can't receive them, read them, or respond to them until you have an account set up. That requires a username and password. Once you're set up, you can send and receive emails without bouncing. It's really quite simple. Just requires a couple of steps that will take only a moment or two."

"Well, I don't have time to fiddle around with small details. Forget email. I'll send my friends a postcard." And with that the elderly gentleman got up and walked away.

TECH TIP

Some seniors are too proud to ask for help. If that's you, let go of your unwillingness and allow someone in the know to show you what to do.

Reflection

*Pride brings a person low, but the lowly
in spirit gain honor* (Proverbs 29:23).

Contemplation

"A proud man is always looking down on things and people;
and, of course, as long as you are looking down,
you cannot see something that is above you."

C.S. Lewis

Timely Prayer

Lord, help me embrace a teachable spirit.

30

Right or Left?

Jeannie's son George donated his old computer to his mother. He wanted her to enjoy the wonders of the Internet and exchange email with family members. He set up the machine and gave his mom a short-and-fast course in the basics of how to use it. All she really needed was instructions on how to log on, get to the Internet, and access email. By the time he finished, he felt great about how much his mother was able to take in and apply. He sat next to her the whole time, of course.

Suddenly she looked at him and blurted out her concern. "I don't get why the applications are on the bottom of the screen. On Maggie's Mac computer, they're on the left. I need a Mac if this is going to work for me."

"Mom, it doesn't really matter. You can open them no matter where they're located. See?" George illustrated by clicking on two icons and opening the programs.

"George, you don't get it. Your mother—ahem—is left-handed." She wagged her left hand in front of his face.

George pecked her on the cheek. "Go ahead and click on any one of the programs—using your left hand."

"Oh, my word! It works either way—right or left hand. How clever."

TECH TIP

Technology doesn't play favorites when it comes to left- or right-handedness.

Reflection

*If any of you lacks wisdom, you should ask God,
who gives generously to all without finding fault,
and it will be given to you* (James 1:5).

Contemplation

"Life is too short to worry about anything."

Eric Davis

Timely Prayer

Lord, you replace my worry with trust in you. Thank you!

Fun Quiz #2

Connect the word to its definition.

1. Keyboard   Device to move a cursor on a computer

2. Mouse   Update the display on a computer screen

3. Laptop   Storage space on a computer

4. Hard drive   Panel of keys to operate a computer

5. Kindle   Electronic device for reading books

6. Dashboard   Short message sent via Twitter

7. Refresh   Telephone service via the Internet

8. Tweet   Graphical display of computer programs

9. Skype   Computer networking environment

10. Cyberspace   Lightweight, portable computer

ANSWERS

1. Panel of keys to operate a computer; 2. Device to move a cursor on a computer; 3. Lightweight, portable computer; 4. Storage space on a computer; 5. Electronic device for reading books; 6. Graphical display of computer programs; 7. Update the display on a computer screen; 8. Short message sent via Twitter; 9. Telephone service via the Internet; 10. Computer networking environment

Email Mishaps

31

Lasting Impression

Linda attended a writers conference one weekend in Nashville, Tennessee. She was so excited to meet famous authors and editors. If she got the opportunity to bump into one in the elevator or sit with one at lunch, she'd pitch her article idea. She knew how important it was to behave in a professional manner and make a good impression to encourage an editor to purchase one of her articles. She'd already communicated with a couple professionals via email to get submission guidelines and recommended topics.

Sure enough, an opportunity popped up. There in person—just inches from the table where she was sitting—stood James Watkins, an acquisitions editor for a Christian publishing house and an editor for a Christian magazine, chatting with an attendee. Linda remembered she was on his email list for updated submission guidelines and article topics. She waited until the gentleman moved away from James, and then she walked right up to him, shook his hand, and reminded him of who she was. She said she looked forward to sending him some ideas for articles based on the topics his magazine preferred. She received a cordial response and the two parted.

Soon after the conference, Linda sent an email to her son, also named James, congratulating him on an accomplishment at work. She expressed her unfathomable love for him too.

"A couple days later," Linda shared, "a thought jumped into my head from out of nowhere." She hadn't heard back from her son, and she got that sick feeling in her stomach that comes when a person commits a big blooper. *Surely I didn't click on the wrong James in my email address book...or did I?* Linda went to her computer, brought up her email account, and checked her email "Sent" file. Yes, she had made that mistake.

"I couldn't imagine what Mr. Watkins thought at the time, but he graciously responded to my apology."

Linda did make a lasting impression on an editor—just not in the way she'd hoped. And, fortunately, she didn't hear from *Mrs.* Watkins.

TECH TIP

Check the "To" box carefully before hitting "Send"—especially if you have more than one James, Joan, Jack, Jill, or other names in your email address book.

Reflection

The Spirit God gave us does not make us timid, but gives us power, love and self-discipline (2 Timothy 1:7).

Contemplation

"To err is human and to blame it on a computer is even more so."

ROBERT ORBEN

Timely Prayer

Lord, thanks for pulling me through embarrassing moments. Help me slow down when I'm rushing around.

32

Email Canada Style

Judy worked in retail in Canada for many years. She was familiar with all the ups and downs involved when dealing with customers. There were often forms to fill in, addresses to verify, and mailing instructions to carry out—depending on what the buyer wanted. She also knew that Canadian postal codes all start with the letter "E." For example: E2H 3B6.

One day an elderly lady came into the store and asked to enroll in the store's reward program.

Judy brought up the details and requirements on her computer. She entered the woman's name, phone number, and address. When it came to the lady's email address, Judy had to stifle a chuckle. She'd asked, "Ma'am, may I have your email address, please, so I can send you a confirmation of enrollment?"

The customer didn't hesitate: "My email? E3H 2B7."

Judy decided in this case it probably would work best to send the confirmation by snail mail.

TECH TIP

Jot down your email address, home address, and phone number on a card and keep it in your purse or wallet so you'll have them handy when you need them. Do not include your password on this list.

Reflection

[Jesus said,] "Come to me, all you who are weary and burdened, and I will give you rest" (Matthew 11:28).

Contemplation

"Science and technology revolutionize our lives, but memory, tradition and myth frame our response."

ARTHUR M. SCHLESINGER

Timely Prayer

Thank you, Lord, for being my "Rememberer" when I forget.

33

Yellow Pages

Chuck admits he's from the old school of technology, back when computer mainframes took up an entire room. He recalls the large cabinets that housed the central processing units and main memories of early computers. "It's hard to believe the little pipsqueaks today can do an adequate job."

"You should try one and see how powerful it is," said his grandson Luke, promising to shop for a laptop with him. "Just think, Gramps, you'll be able to post photos, send notes to your friends and family using email, and you can get answers to just about any question you have by typing in the search box on Google a few key words related to the topic. I can show you. I think you'll love it. No more 'yellow pages' for you."

Chuck knew Luke wanted him to get with the program and stop leaning on old technology and print sources. Every time Chuck wanted to find a store or a restaurant, he'd turn to the yellow pages in the phone book. It took a lot of time and energy, and sometimes the information was outdated and the shop or dinner house had gone out of business.

"What do you think, Grandpa?" Luke asked, nudging his grandfather's elbow.

"Oh, all right, but not right now. I have to think a little more about it. I'll let you know in the morning."

Luke knew when to let go. He said good night and left for home.

The following morning Luke called his grandfather and asked if he was ready to shop with him for a computer.

"Sure, why not?" Chuck grumbled. "Time to bite the bullet."

The pair purchased a laptop later that morning. Luke set it up, showing his grandfather how easy it was to use and how useful Google can be when he wanted to find a specific place or get an answer to a question.

Chuck listened but didn't have much to say in return.

Luke decided to give his grandpa time and check back the next day. The following afternoon he stopped by Chuck's house. "How's it going?" he asked.

Chuck frowned. "Not so well. I think the yellow pages are far superior to your friend Google."

"How so?"

"Because they are organized by category, and items are listed in alphabetical order. Google, on the other hand, is all over the map. I typed in the word *restaurants* and there were listings for eating establishments as far away as Hong Kong. Now why would I want to fly around the world for a steak and a baked potato?"

Luke chuckled. Clearly his grandfather needed a few more tutoring lessons. But he had faith in the old man. He'd get his grandpa up to speed in no time. But first he had to help him recover from his yellow page addiction.

TECH TIP

If you prefer the yellow pages, there is a print edition of "Internet Yellow Pages." You can purchase it through Amazon.com.

Reflection

The Lord is my helper; I will not be afraid (Hebrews 13:6).

Contemplation

"I am thankful the most important key in history was invented.
It's not the key to your house, your car, your boat,
your safety deposit box, your bike lock,
or your private community. It's the key to
order, sanity, and peace of mind. The key is 'Delete.'"

ELAYNE BOOSLER

Timely Prayer

I may want to "delete" many of the messages I receive
on my computer, Lord, but I will always "save" and obey
whatever word you send me.

34

Creative Spelling

Earl looked at his great-granddaughter Jenny holding her laptop computer as she visited him in his room at Shady Oaks Senior Living. He slapped his forehead in animated confusion. "What do you mean by the 'Internet'? I've heard of interchanges—freeways coming together; interfere—getting in the way of something or someone, but I don't know Internet. Does it mean between two nets like in tennis?"

Jenny smiled. "No, Gramps, not exactly. About forty years ago, the term 'Internet' was kind of shorthand for the technical computer term 'internetwork.' People were able to connect with each other through computers and also get information they needed." Jenny could tell by the expression on her gramp's face that she'd lost him a sentence or two ago.

"You can do that with telephones and the telephone book. I use them all the time."

"Yes, and that still works, but the Internet is faster and easier and can give so much more information."

Earl's eyes opened wide and he leaned forward. "Can you show me?"

"Sure!" Jenny pulled up the website for Shady Oaks Senior Living. "See? Now anyone with a computer can look for info about this place and find out where it is, the cost of living here, and what benefits it offers."

Earl shook his head. "Well, I'll be." He talked about the first phone, the first television set, and the first typewriter he owned, but a computer and the Internet? "Looks like I'm behind the times, my dear." He settled back in his easy chair.

"How do you know how to get where you're going without a map?" he asked.

"I type into this little search box a few words that tell the computer what info I need, and then up pops a list of places where I can go to find what I'm looking for. When I saw the U-R-L, the link, for Shady Oaks Senior Living, I clicked on it and this is what I got—the pictures you see here."

Earl pointed a gnarled finger at the screen. "So this is an Url?"

"Actually, it's not a word, just three letters: U-R-L. They stand for 'Uniform Resource Locator,' but you don't have to remember the definition—just what it does."

Earl chuckled. "I kind of like calling it 'Url.' Sounds like my name. Who'd have thought that something on the Internet would have the same name I do—even though they got the spelling wrong."

Jenny laughed. Enough computer education for one day! She poured them cups of tea, and they sat back and talked about her latest marathon race. Earl was very interested in that subject because he'd been a runner in his youth.

TECH TIP

It takes some time, but even technophobes can learn how to find information on the Internet.

Reflection

If you forgive other people when they sin against you,
your heavenly Father will also forgive you (Matthew 6:14).

Contemplation

"The Internet is becoming the town square for
the global village of tomorrow."

BILL GATES

Timely Prayer

Thanks, dear God, for the "magic" of being able to communicate across the globe in ways I never dreamed possible just decades ago.

35

Email Shemail

Larry had just about had it with email. He hadn't wanted to get involved with it in the first place, but his daughter Kendra talked him into it so he could stay in touch with family and friends. Phone calls were becoming more difficult because of his hearing loss, and his fingers got tired when writing longhand. So he went along with Kendra. But he had no idea at the time that soon he'd be bombarded with unwanted emails from all sorts of vendors and businesses. Some of them he'd never even heard of until their ad popped into his inbox.

"Kendra, this email isn't working for me. I don't have time to write back to all these people. Who are they anyway?"

"Dad, you can rest easy. Just delete the ones you don't want and move on to the ones you do want to read. I know it's a pain, but unfortunately that's the way it is these days. We get unwanted advertising flyers in our mailboxes and stuck in our doors. It's the same with the Internet. You can't stop all the ads, so just drag them into the trash, similar to what you do with paper ads."

"I resent that these fellas think they can unload on me without asking, and then it becomes my job to get rid of what they send." Larry let out a puff of air and shook his head. "Doesn't do much good anyway. They're right back the next day—and in my face."

Kendra sympathized with her dad and agreed with him. She didn't like the spam any more than her father did.

The next day Larry opened his email account and aside from a message from his granddaughter and an invitation for coffee from a good buddy, there was nothing of interest. Most of it was junk that he now had to delete. One ad, however, caught his attention because of a message in tiny print. It said "Click here to unsubscribe, fill in the blanks, and we'll take you off our list."

"Good idea!" Larry mumbled after clicking on the link. He didn't recall having subscribed in the first place, but it didn't matter. He was happy to get this company off his list and his email address off their list.

A second later a message box popped up. There was a space for his email address, so he filled that in, and then filled in the second space with his user name. Easy enough. He typed in Larry Joseph Logan. A new screen opened saying his user name was incorrect and to please try again.

"No way!" he shouted at the screen. "A man would know his own name, wouldn't he? I've been Larry Joseph Logan now for going on 85 years." With that he closed the computer and decided to give it back to Kendra on her next visit.

TECH TIP

When you get frustrated with unwanted email, take a deep breath, smile, and move on. Delete or unsubscribe to what you don't want without hesitation. No need to waste your time when you never subscribed in the first place.

Reflection

Let us not become weary in doing good (Galatians 6:9).

Contemplation

"I'm pretty sure people are going to start writing
letters again once the email fad passes."

WILLIE GEIST

Timely Prayer

Lord, it's a good thing I never have to give up on communicating with you.

36

Sorry About That

Ben is no longer a party animal. In fact, he's far from it. In his younger years he liked to chugalug with the best of them, but not anymore. He's retired to a quiet routine that includes reading, doing a bit of gardening, going to church, and keeping up with family and close friends. Occasionally he considers attending a shindig—if it's close to home.

One Tuesday afternoon, his friend Jim called and asked him over for coffee, dessert, and a game of cards the following Saturday evening. Ben said yes right away. The get-together sounded like something he'd enjoy. Not too many folks, just a little food, and a friendly game to stimulate his mind.

Wednesday, Thursday, and Friday of that week came and went, and suddenly it was Saturday. Ben went to the supermarket as was his custom, took a little snooze after a late lunch, and then walked the neighborhood for his daily exercise. By six o'clock, he was feeling tired so he relaxed for a couple of hours in front of the television and then went to bed. Suddenly he awakened at three, remembering that he'd forgotten to go to Jim's house for the dessert and card game.

He piled out of bed and checked his cell phone, which he'd switched off earlier in the evening. Sure enough, there was a text from his friend, who was wondering what had happened to him.

Bill couldn't sleep another minute until he returned the text with a sincere apology. He typed as quickly as he could with one finger and no glasses. Then he pressed "Send," and his message sailed off to Jim. Bill went back to bed and slept till late morning.

He awoke and checked his phone for messages, hoping Jim had read his text about the night before and responded. Yep, he had:

> Bill, no problem. We missed you, but my son stepped in and played for you. Very sorry to hear about your incontinence. In that case, maybe it's just as well you didn't make it last night. We'll try again. By the way, there is no shame in wearing adult diapers. No one has to know but you.

"What?" Bill wondered what had gotten into Jim's head. Maybe his text was meant for someone else. Bill reread his own message, wondering what he could have typed that led Jim to such a conclusion. There it was in plain English:

> Hi, Jim. Bill here. Sorry I missed the evening at your house. I apologize for my incontinence.

Incontinence! That was supposed to be *any inconvenience.* Auto-correct had done it again. Bill laughed and then phoned Jim. He wanted to set the record straight.

TECH TIP

It pays to reread all your texts *before* hitting "Send." Auto-correct can be a wild card.

Reflection

Great peace have those who love your law, and nothing can make them stumble (Psalm 119:165).

Contemplation

"Computers have enabled people to make more mistakes faster than almost any invention in history."

MITCH RATCLIFFE

Timely Prayer

Lord, I can see that a sense of humor is essential if I'm to get through old age.

37

A Bunch of Characters

Rita received a notice from her email server that the company was conducting a password audit to be sure everyone had safe entry to their site when picking up email. There had been some tampering by an unknown source, so the president of the company suggested that to be on the safe side everyone should create new passwords.

Oh, dear! That meant Rita had to think of a new one—just when she was feeling comfortable remembering the one she had. But, hey, she didn't want to experience a breach in her security, so she followed the instructions for creating a new password—eight characters long and including at least one capital letter. It was a bit of a chore, to say the least, to think up eight characters she would readily remember, but she did it.

Shortly afterward, she received an email from the company saying that they'd received her new password, but they were curious as to why it was so long. "Won't it be difficult to remember so many words? If you'd like to change it again, that would be fine."

Rita frowned. *Why should they care about my password as long as I'm happy with it and it meets their criteria?* She looked at her password again, checking to be sure she'd followed the instructions: SupermanBatmanSpidermanTomJerryFelixGoofyWoody. Yep! Right on. Eight characters and at least one capital letter.

TECH TIP

Some suggestions, even instructions, aren't meant to be taken literally.

Reflection

*Light shines on the righteous and
joy on the upright in heart* (Psalm 97:11).

Contemplation

"If you don't know how to do something, you
don't know how to do it with a computer."

AUTHOR UNKNOWN

Timely Prayer

Lord, I'm noticing that when I feel stuck or confused, I don't usually need a tech manual. I just need your wisdom and guidance.

38

Gee! Mail!

Irma winced at the sight of her daughter Gail running up the stairs to the apartment. She knew she was in for it. Gail would start pressuring her again to open an email account so the two could contact each other frequently and easily, especially now that Irma was having trouble hearing. Although Irma liked the idea of typing messages instead of calling and getting Gail's voice mail, which was happening more and more these days now that Gail was working full-time, Irma was a bit apprehensive. She had her new laptop, but she hadn't done much with it.

"Mom, I'll handle everything. I promise. You can sit beside me while I set up the account. You can pick your email address and your password, so it's entirely yours, okay? It's as simple as pie."

Irma laughed. "I never was any good at baking pies, so don't tell me that."

Gail kissed her mother on the cheek. "Mom, please. Don't you want to be part of the twenty-first century? Keep up with the times? Stay current? And it would be a big help to Brady and me. We can stay in touch with you any hour of the day."

Irma sighed. "Okay, I'll give it a try—but I'm not making any promises. I'm not too swift at learning new information at my age."

Gail smiled, patted her mother's hand, and opened her mom's laptop. "I think it's best if we get you a gmail account. It's very popular and easy to set up. Okay, here we are. Now I'll need some information from you. What address would you like to use?"

"What do you mean? Like it's a choice? I've lived here at 102 Northside Avenue for fifty years, and you're asking me what address I'd like?"

"I meant what address would you like to use for your email account?" Gail let out a long breath. This was going to take more time than she'd hoped.

TECH TIP

It helps to become familiar with tech terminology so you'll know what people are talking about when they help you do computer work.

Reflection

The testing of your faith produces perseverance (James 1:3).

Contemplation

"To me, emails are a little bit frustrating."

T. BOONE PICKENS

Timely Prayer

Lord, I'm grateful that whether or not I ever get computer-savvy, you never ignore me.

39

Email Bail

Brendon worked for a well-known email service company. He prided himself on his ability to gently handle cranky customers who called in complaining about not being able to download their email. One man in particular appeared to have a huge problem, so Brendon bent over backward troubleshooting. He helped the client verify his settings on his end and Brendon did the same at his end. Finally, Brendon realized the only hope was to have the customer close the account and start all over. But that didn't solve the problem either.

"I'm getting a message that says 'can't connect to the server.' So I'm wondering if you're having issues," said the customer.

"Actually we're not, sir. If we were," Brendon joked, "we'd be having many more callers this morning. All right, let's try an alternate incoming server address and see if that works."

Brendon listened as the customer typed.

"Nope. Still can't connect," the man said.

"Hmmm. This seems impossible. Are you able to load any Internet pages—you know such as a new channel or Facebook or any other link you're interested in? Do they come up on your screen when you type in the address?"

"No, I can't load any pages. Our ISP is having a power outage right now."

Brendon let out a long breath. "Well, there's your problem. Unfortunately, without an Internet connection you won't be able to get email."

"You're joking! You just want to get me off the phone, don't you? What does the Internet have to do with email anyway?"

"Sir, trust me. It has everything to do with email. I suggest you wait until the power outage is repaired, and then I'm sure your email will download perfectly."

"Well, okay, if I have to."

"Have a nice day, and thank you for calling."

TECH TIP

Even some basic knowledge of how email and the Internet relate can save you a lot of problems and embarrassment. Might be time for a beginner's course at a local college, library, or community center.

Reflection

The LORD lifts up those who are bowed down (Psalm 146:8).

Contemplation

"Technology should have freed mankind from the burdens of life. Instead, it created new ones."

BRIAN HERBERT AND KEVIN J. ANDERSON

Timely Prayer

Lord, the more I learn the behinder I get!

40

I've Got Mail

Maggie called the support desk for help. She knew enough to do that whenever she ran into problems with her computer. In fact, that's why she purchased an extended service agreement. It would be just like her to get in a fix and not be able to get out of it on her own. This computer stuff was pretty new to her, but she was determined to learn and do as much as possible. Maggie would not be overcome by technology. After all, she was a college graduate.

"Ma'am, how can I help you this morning? My name is George, and I'm here to serve."

"Oh, George! I'm so glad you're on duty today. You helped me one other time, and you were absolutely right on. I did everything you told me to do and, bingo! it worked."

"Well, thank you. My pleasure. What seems to be the problem today?"

"I've tried and tried this morning to open my email, and it simply won't come up. I don't understand."

"Well let's start with your ISP. What I mean is, who is your Internet Service Provider—the company that makes it possible for you to have a connection to the Internet? If they're having a problem, such as an electrical outage, that could be causing your email to fail to load."

Oh, dear! Such a lot of tech talk. Maggie's head was swimming. She paused trying to think of what to say next.

"Ma'am, are you there?"

"I'm not sure." She wrinkled her brow, willing the answer to spring from her mouth. Then suddenly it hit her. "My ISP...I think it's 'You've Got Mail.'"

TECH TIP

You've Got Mail is a movie titled after the announcement AOL email users hear when they get mail in their inbox.

Reflection

Whoever heeds discipline shows
the way to life (Proverbs 10:17).

Contemplation

"One look at an email can rob you of
15 minutes of focus."

JACQUELINE LEO

Timely Prayer

Lord, you are so good to me, helping me through my confusion so I can find the truth.

Fun Quiz #3

Circle the correct answer for each of these statements.

1. In an email address, the symbol @ means *at*.   T F

2. Firefox, Google Chrome, and IE are
   types of web browsers.   T F

3. The word "laptop" refers to a computer that can
   only be used on your lap.   T F

4. URL refers to a particular computer model.   T F

5. Gmail is a type of email.   T F

6. ISP stands for Internet Service Problem.   T F

7. Megabyte and gigabyte mean roughly the same thing.   T F

8. "Mail merge" is sorting through all your emails
   after a vacation.   T F

9. "Times New Roman" is a book about
   modern-day Rome.   T F

10. A computer monitor is a display device.   T F

1, 2, 5, 10 are true; 3, 4, 6, 7, 8, 9 are false.

ANSWERS

103

Smartphone Foibles

41

India Jones

Heather's husband, Leo, recently turned seventy. He retired some time ago so he has no interest or, according to him, no need for all this "e-stuff." "No thanks," he says to email, smartphones, Google, e-readers, and URLs. He has an old cell phone, but he rarely turns it on, so Heather can't reach him when he's away even if she wanted or needed to.

However, when he expressed a desire to go on a mission trip to India with a medical team from church, Heather decided to buy Leo an iPad so he could take photos and stay in touch with her by email. Leo let out a big sigh when she told him. She sensed his resistance, but she persisted. "I'll feel better if we can communicate at least a few times while you're gone. You can even use the Internet to make a phone call using Skype, a free calling and video service. I'll show you how easy it is to use the iPad. Nothing to it."

Leo nodded but rolled his eyes.

When the iPad arrived, Leo surrendered to his wife's tutoring.

"I spent lots of time training him," said Heather. "By the time he left for the trip, he was pretty much up to speed."

One day, however, the iPad froze while Leo was overseas. He didn't know what was wrong or how to fix it, and neither did any of his travel mates. So he called Heather in the United States to get some tech support. The iPad needed a *hard start*, she told him. It was an easy fix, involving shutting down the tablet, unplugging it for a few seconds, and starting it up again. In a matter of minutes Leo and his iPad were up and running.

While on the phone, Heather started laughing. She suddenly realized what a funny situation this was. "Leo, do you realize that you're making a call to me in the United States *from* India for tech support? Now that's a switch!"

Leo laughed too. He recounted some of the times Heather had received tech support from a tech rep in India. "At least I understand *your* accent," he said.

TECH TIP

When in a tech dilemma, don't panic. If you can access the Internet, type into Google what you need or want, and then click. More options than you can possibly use will pop up immediately.

Reflection

[Jesus] said to his disciples, "Why are you so afraid?
Do you still have no faith?" (Mark 4:40).

Contemplation

"The Internet: transforming society and shaping
the future through chat."

DAVE BARRY

Timely Prayer

Lord, thanks for being my ultimate tech guy. You always steer me in the right direction for the perfect answer to my problems.

42

Charge!

Barbara's mother, Margaret, decided to take a seven-day trip to visit her sister Rose, who was newly widowed. The two made plans to spend part of the week at a spa where they could swim and enjoy massages and facials. The rest of the time they'd take bus rides to explore the new surroundings. They were ready to leave their routines behind for a few days and simply enjoy each other's company. Rose had been through a lot and needed some fun.

Barbara agreed it was a wonderful idea and offered to help her mother pack and then drive her to the bus terminal the following week.

Margaret was afraid of flying and didn't want to drive, so the Greyhound bus seemed the ideal option. On the day of departure, Barbara picked up her mother, lifted the heavy suitcase into the trunk of her car, and off they went. She'd put together a special bag of snacks, a sandwich, a bottle of water, and a candy bar for her mom to enjoy on the long bus ride. She wanted her mother to be comfortable and well fed.

"Mom, do you want me to go with you? I mean you're not so young anymore. I'm worried you might need help."

Margaret batted the air with a free hand. "No, I don't want you going with me. I'd feel like a schoolgirl on the first day of class with her mother hovering over her." She frowned. "I can take care of myself. I'm going to relax and have fun, and that's it. You have your family to think of. Trust me on this. Have I ever given you reason to doubt my thinking?"

"Well…" Barbara wisely decided not to say what was on her mind at that moment. Her mom had left the stove on a couple of times, but she did catch it before the kitchen caught fire. And she'd forgotten to turn off the hose one afternoon so it flooded the front lawn, but no permanent damage was done. A neighbor saw what happened and turned off the spigot.

Barbara just had to ask one more question or she wouldn't rest. "Mom, do you have your cell phone with you?" She wanted to be certain they could get in touch with each other if something unexpected occurred. "Mom, do you have your cell phone with you?" she repeated.

"Yes."

"What about the charger? Do you have that too?"

"Yes, but I won't need it. I only turn on my phone if there's an emergency."

"But what if *I* have an emergency?" Barbara asked. "I'll want to call you, and your phone will be off."

"Oh! Well, just look at the paper on my kitchen table. It lists all the places we'll be visiting."

Barbara slapped her forehead gently in exasperation, kissed her mom goodbye, and said a quick prayer that everything would be all right.

TECH TIP

If you have a cell phone, charge it every evening. Keep it handy day and night. This may seem like obvious advice, but many people forget to charge their phones, so when they most need them they're out of juice.

Reflection

Do not fear, for I am with you (Isaiah 41:10).

Contemplation

"Apparently we love our own cell phones, but
we hate everyone else's."

Joe Bob Briggs

Timely Prayer

Dear God, I'm grateful I can depend on you—especially when my cell phone goes out.

43

Upgrade Upset

Doris drove to the phone store. She'd heard about the new upgrade available for her cell phone brand and wanted to keep up with the times. No problem. The salesman was more than willing to accommodate her. In fact, he sold her a smartphone and took her "dumb" phone as a trade-in.

What a nice man. Doris liked the attention she received and all the helpful information he provided, though he talked a bit fast and she had to turn up her hearing aid to catch all the new words he tossed her way.

But no worries. This phone would do practically everything she wanted with the press of a finger or thumb. The phone even had a friendly woman named Siri who spoke to her with a simple press of the button below the screen. "May I help you?" She was so polite and helpful that Doris spoke to her often. Siri told her the location of the closest gas station or the nearest coffee house. Doris had found a smart new friend.

But when it came to phone calls, Doris had a bit more to learn. She began calling her daughter Caroline several times a day, saying, "I see that you called."

"No, Mom, actually I didn't. Is anything wrong?" Caroline soon became worried.

Her mom replied, "I think so. *Your* phone seems to be acting up. I see your name and phone number here plain as day, but you're telling me you didn't call. What's that about?"

"Mom, I bet you're looking at the list of calls you made instead of calls you missed."

Doris took a minute to study her phone. Sure enough, her daughter was right. Doris was too embarrassed to admit it. "Whatever," she replied. "If you haven't called me, then why not? The least you could do is call your mom once a day and check in."

"Will do, Mom. Will do. Sorry about that. I love you."

TECH TIP

When you upgrade your old phone to a new one, be sure you understand what you're getting, how to use it, and, more importantly, what you're paying for. Then ask yourself if the financial investment is worth the amount of time needed to use all the gizmos that come with it.

Reflection

Those who know your name trust in you, for you, LORD,
have never forsaken those who seek you (Psalm 9:10).

Contemplation

"It used to be that we imagined that our mobile phones would
be for us to talk to each other.
Now, our mobile phones are there to talk to us."

SHERRY TURKLE

Timely Prayer

Dear God, thank you that I can reach you anytime day
or night—and I don't need a cell phone to do it.

44

Outside Her Comfort Zone

Josie finally felt comfortable with her cell phone after resisting getting the device for many a moon. Then a newer, better, and zippier version came on the market. Should she ignore it or buy it and learn how to use it? Such a dilemma. Surely there were more important things to take up her time than puzzling over a new cell phone.

"In my childhood home," she said, "our phone was black and hung on the wall. To call someone you had to dial the number. You also had to stand up to use it. It was a party line. If it rang three times, we knew someone was calling our family. Most people who had phones then knew what to do with them since they all were pretty much the same. Except for color, location, and eventually push buttons, phones didn't change much."

It was clear that Josie liked the good old days when technology seemed simpler. But the old phone couldn't do all that the new one could. And the new one was compact and lightweight, perfect for pocket, purse, or belt. A person could take it everywhere. "I resisted longer than most," admitted Josie. "Eventually I surrendered because even pay phones became scarce. If I was on the road and needed to make a call, I couldn't find a pay phone for miles. I remember nearly panicking when I had car trouble once."

Josie gave in and purchased a cell phone. "Once I figured out the basics, I kept it into antiquity, only giving it up when a broken hinge threatened to separate me from my contacts."

The next step for Josie felt like a quantum leap. She bought a smartphone. "After two-and-a-half years, I felt pretty smart and comfortable using it. That is, until Costco/Verizon made my husband and me an offer we couldn't refuse. We upgraded to phones the company paid each of us $100 to take. Suddenly I wasn't quite as smart. But now, after several months, I'm almost back to where I was with the one I replaced."

So much work and so much time! Josie is adamant against any more changes. "Don't talk to me about upgrading in the near future," she said. "I need to settle in for a while."

Like many people, Josie likes to feel "comfortable and competent" with what she uses. "Is that a sign of getting old? Or is it just my personality?" she asked. "I guess if I don't *have* to do it, and can take my time, and decide to enjoy the journey of relearning, it might happen. But right now I'd rather be doing something else."

TECH TIP

Don't feel pressured to keep up with the latest cell phone technology. If the phone you have works and you like it, stick with it.

Reflection

Put your hope in God (Psalm 42:11).

Contemplation

"Now we're e-mailing and tweeting and texting so much,
a phone call comes as a fresh surprise."

Susan Orlean

Timely Prayer

Lord, how comforting to know that I can reach you whenever and however I wish. You are always on call.

45

Pay as You Go—or No!

According to Margie, phones are now "pay as you go—or *no*." She and her sister, Paula, each have a decent phone that works without having to have contracts or countless bells and whistles. They can phone family members and friends whenever they want without making any mistakes because the devices are so easy to use. The learning curve is nil—just the way they like it.

Paula's grown daughters, on the other hand, took the opposite approach. They each have the latest tech tools on their phones: Internet access, instant messaging, video, a camera, games, and even 3-D visuals. They finally convinced their mother that she too should purchase a smartphone and get with the times. What fun they could have exchanging photos, posting pictures to messages and Facebook, and looking up information on the Internet whenever and wherever. And while waiting in a doctor's office or in line at the post office, their mom could play some fun games like Wordfeud and Scrabble.

Paula agreed, though reluctantly. She did want to stay up-to-date with her busy daughters and grandkids. But, alas, after a few weeks of fiddling with the preferences and settings, she returned the phone to the store and stated emphatically, "I feel like a dummy, so I want my dumb phone back."

TECH TIP

Sometimes it's just as well to leave things as they are—especially if everything is working.

Reflection

In Christ you have been brought to fullness (Colossians 2:10).

Contemplation

"I use an outdated cell phone, and I'm fine with it."
NICOLAS CAGE

Timely Prayer

Dear God, I'm glad that technology never interferes with my communication with you.

46

Out in the Cold

Helen's mom and dad gave in and bought a cell phone for emergencies and to use when they're away from home. They admit it's a bit of a pain to use since they live in a remote area where it's difficult to get good cell reception indoors. They prefer their landline. They've had it for years, and it's reliable. The couple is also thrifty with their money, so they use the cell to call Helen because long-distance calls are part of their package.

"On the other hand," Helen said with a twinkle in her eye, "conversations in the winter between my parents and me are short and to the point because Mom has to stand outside on the porch to make the connection."

"I'll keep this brief," says her mother after a moment or two. "I'm outside, and I'm getting cold."

Helen likes to joke in return. "Okay, Mom, 'bye for now. We'll catch up on all the news in the spring."

TECH TIP

If you can't get good reception, consider buying a booster so you can. Check with your cell phone service provider or, if necessary, switch providers.

Reflection

You will call, and the Lord will answer (Isaiah 58:9).

Contemplation

"Cell phones are so convenient that they're an inconvenience."

HARUKI MURAKAMI

Timely Prayer

I'm never out in the cold when it comes to talking with you, dear Lord. I love that.

47

I Just Don't Get It

Ruthie looked at her cell phone and then her iPad. Her son Rich kept her up-to-date with all these gizmos and gadgets, but she couldn't keep them all straight. After all, she came from an era when all one had was a black manual typewriter and a black phone on the wall. She never did learn to type very well, so how did Rich expect her to start now? But she didn't want to disappoint him, so she tried her best to catch up whenever he stopped by to give her a lesson.

"Mom, it's really not difficult once you get the hang of it," he often said. "You just have to concentrate and think about what you want to do."

"I want to give it all up, that's what," she'd mumble under her breath.

"Look, Mom," Rich persisted, "you can contact me any time of the day or night with a text message through your cell phone. I'll write a sample, and you can watch."

Rich proceeded to click on "Message" on his phone, type in his mother's phone number, and then type in a short text in a little box: "Hi Mom. It's Rich. I love you."

He clicked "Send" and off it went. A moment later, Ruthie's phone dinged. Rich showed her how to retrieve the message.

Ruthie smiled. It looked easy and seemed like fun.

"Now you try it," said Rich.

Ruthie put in her son's phone number, which she'd memorized after all these years, and then typed her message. It took her a while but she got it done: "Hi Son. Love you too." She pressed "Send," and her message flew into cyberspace. A moment later, Rich picked up the message on his phone.

"Great job, Mom! See? I told you there was nothing to it. You can send me an email message too—on your phone or on your iPad. Let's practice that."

Ruthie and Rich spent a few more minutes reviewing what to do on each device. Then Rich left for work and said he'd check back later.

Ruthie collapsed on the sofa after all this learning. She was exhausted. Later that day she decided to try again. First, she'd surprise Rich with an email using her iPad. She opened the email program. So far so good. Then she typed into the "To" box the name of her son's company, since she wanted to reach him at work WonderSupplies. She wrote her short message and then hit "Send." It didn't work. An error message popped up. "No such address." What had Rich told her to do? She couldn't remember. How come she could send a message on the cell phone but not on the iPad?

Ruthie had had it. She picked up the phone in the kitchen—the one plugged into the wall—and called her son. "I'm done," she said with a huff. "I don't get all this tech stuff. Please come and pick up this iPad and give it to your daughter. If you and I want to talk, let's meet for coffee—where I can see your face and kiss you in person."

TECH TIP

Sometimes an in-person meeting beats a text and an email, especially if that person is someone you love.

Reflection

Let perseverance finish its work so that you may be mature and complete, not lacking anything (James 1:4).

Contemplation

"A computer makes it possible to do, in half an hour, tasks which were completely unnecessary to do before."

AUTHOR UNKNOWN

Timely Prayer

Dear God, I'm thinking if I spent even half the time in prayer that I spend on the computer, I'd be a spiritual giant!

48

You Call This Customer Service?

Bert phoned the number on the card he'd received from the customer rep that set up Bert's computer and smartphone so he could pick up email on both devices.

"If you need assistance," the young man had said before leaving Bert's house, "just call this number, and someone will be glad to help."

Today was the day Bert needed all the help he could get. His smartphone seemed pretty dumb to him. It wouldn't deliver email the way it was supposed to.

"Customer service. How may I assist you?" The cheery voice on the other end of the line boosted Bert's confidence that someone could get him out of this jam.

"I'm not getting my emails on my phone," Bert barked. He didn't mean to be rude but he was pretty annoyed.

"Did you type in your password first?" the cheery voice asked.

"What's my password?" Bert wanted to cut the "Q & A" and get to the bottom line.

"I don't know, sir." The cheery voice lowered. "It would be the one you chose when you set up your email account."

"I didn't set it up! One of your reps did. So how should I know? Ask him."

"Sir, a password is private. It's for your protection so no one can bring in your email without your permission. The rep would have asked you to choose a password, and he would look away when you typed it in. Most likely he suggested you make a note of it somewhere so you could retrieve it in case you forgot it."

"Fine. So now what? I don't remember choosing one."

"You can change it. No problem. I'll send you an email, which you can pick up on your computer. Follow the instructions for changing your password. Then use that one for both your phone and your computer and you should have no problem. Oh, and sir, you might want to write down the new password and keep it in a safe place."

"So what you're saying is that in order to get email on my phone I have to *change* a password I never had in the first place?"

"You could say it that way. Yes, one way or the other you'll need a new password in order to clear up this problem."

"So it rests on me, does it? And you call this customer service?"

TECH TIP

Actually, it's good that you can choose your own password. Then you know you're protected and no one else can get into your account.

Reflection

Dear friends, let us love one another, for love comes from God (1 John 4:7).

Contemplation

"The human spirit must prevail over technology."

ALBERT EINSTEIN

Timely Prayer

Thank you, Lord, that I don't need a password to contact you.

49

Flippin' Funny

Sally bought her mother a little flip phone to ease her into the twenty-first century. "I taught her what to do with it and watched while she played with the buttons. She was very resistant at first." Sally expected that to change after her mother had a little time to experiment on her own. But it didn't.

One afternoon Sally walked into her mom's house, and just then the phone rang and rang again. Sally got worried. Why didn't her mother answer it? What if something had happened to her? She dashed from room to room calling her name. She found her standing over the bathroom sink with a little black jewelry box opened up and pressed against her ear. She was yelling, "Hello? Hello?"

Sally walked up and touched her mother on the shoulder. "What's up, Mom? Do you need some help? Where's your phone?"

Her mom slammed the box on the counter. "No one's there. The person must have hung up. How rude."

Sally chuckled. She picked up her mother's glasses and handed them to her. "Mom, that was your ring box. Here's your flip phone."

TECH TIP

Keep your cell phone in a handy place—clipped to your belt or in a small pouch around your shoulder or waist—so you won't miss any calls. Your phone will always be with you no matter what.

Reflection

Trust in the LORD (Psalm 37:3).

Contemplation

"Technology can be our best friend, and
technology can also be the biggest
party pooper of our lives."

STEVEN SPIELBERG

Timely Prayer

Sometimes, Lord, the whole tech thing feels overwhelming and the old-fashioned way of communicating feels right.

50

Setting Things Straight

"I'm sorry to hear your phone isn't working." Salesperson Ashley heard the agitation in the customer's voice and hoped to steady the man before he asked to speak to the manager of the phone store. "Have you checked your phone settings, Mr. Jones? You may have turned off the services you want by accident."

"What do you take me for? I certainly did *not* turn off the services—by accident or otherwise. Look, I'm at my brother's house, and the elevation is very high so I made sure to turn the phone to 'airplane mode.' It's really bugging me that my phone isn't working. Now I can't play Wordfeud with my neighbor."

"I'm glad you mentioned that." Ashley was grateful nothing serious had occurred. "Airplane mode disables your phone from using game features and other Internet options. Turn that off, please, and try again."

"I think you're just trying to brush me off, aren't you? How do people talk to each other on airplanes? It seems I know more about this than you do. Pretty frustrating to think you're getting paid to dish out incorrect information."

"Will you explain, please? I'm not sure what you mean by people talking to each other in airplanes."

"You really don't know? Haven't you flown in the last ten years? Airplane mode is for calling someone while up high in the air."

"I'm sorry sir, but that's not what 'airplane mode' is for. It just turns off certain phone features so the electronics won't interfere with anything in the aircraft.

TECH TIP

Read the instructions for any device *before* losing your temper with a customer service agent.

Reflection

[The LORD] mocks proud mockers but shows favor to the humble and oppressed (Proverbs 3:34).

Contemplation

"It has become appallingly obvious that our technology has exceeded our humanity."

ALBERT EINSTEIN

Timely Prayer

God, too often I'm ready to blame someone else for my mistakes and ignorance. Please give me the gift of humility.

51

Wrong Number

Robin waltzed through the front door of her condo and kicked off her shoes. She felt giddy. The man she'd met on ChristianMingle.com was a true gentleman in person. He was even more than she'd hoped for. She pulled out her phone to send him a text. He deserved an extra thank you for such a lovely evening. The food at La Fonda was wonderful, and the walk they took in the park by the moonlight reminded her of former days when she was young, beautiful, and in love with life. Maybe she really could have a second chance.

But then Robin remembered how important it was to play it cool. *Don't gush,* she chided herself. After all, this had been their first real date. Their initial meeting over coffee didn't count because that was just a trial to see if they were a good match. It certainly seemed they were then and even more so now. Robin pulled up the directory, clicked on his name, and typed as quickly as her fingers could move:

> Hey there. I can't thank you enough for the fabulous evening we shared. You made it so special. The food was awesome, and the walk and talk felt so right. Next time it's my turn to plan a surprise evening for you. Till then, Robin.

A few seconds later Robin's phone lit up and chimed. *It must be Ron!* But no, it was a text from a woman who signed off as Val. And she was angry:

> Who do you think you are writing such a personal message to my husband? We share this phone so you can't fool me.

Robin was so taken aback she fell against the wall and sank to her knees. Who was Val? This must be a terrible mistake! Then she checked the name at the top of the text she'd sent. *Oh no!* She'd bared her soul to *Ron Richmond*, a repairman she'd hired to fix a plumbing problem, instead of *Ron Taylor*, her date tonight. How embarrassing! Robin quickly replied to Val and apologized for clicking on the wrong number. As for thanking her date, she decided she'd benefit from a good night's sleep first. From now on she would always wear her reading glasses when texting.

TECH TIP

Always double-check the "To" box before hitting "Send" to avoid embarrassment.

Reflection

You will protect me from trouble (Psalm 32:7).

Contemplation

"You cannot have a positive life and a negative mind."

JOYCE MEYER

Timely Prayer

Lord, when I rush, I make mistakes. When I slow down and check with you first, I make positive choices.

52

Chatty Cathy

Cathy was a novice when it came to technology, but she was willing to learn, especially now that she had a brand-new cell phone. She could hardly wait to use the FaceTime feature with her sister Carla, in Germany. The fact that the long-distance calls were part of the calling plan made the application even more attractive. In the old days, her mom had spent a fortune on international calls to her sister in Spain.

A few days after purchasing her phone and playing with the apps to see what all she could do, Cathy decided to call Carla and surprise her. She chose the hour carefully, realizing there was a nine-hour difference in their time zones.

A few short rings later, Cathy was excited to hear Carla's voice. Her sister asked questions in rapid-fire succession so she could catch up on family news. Cathy held the phone out in front of her and could see Carla's face just fine. How wonderful! Then she put the phone back to her ear to continue the conversation, chatting away without hesitation.

Carla cut in. "Cath, I can't see your face. What's going on at your end?"

Cathy held out the phone again. "I can see yours just fine."

"Okay. Now I see you," said Carla.

Cathy tucked her phone beside her ear again and carried on.

"Wait. You're gone again. Are you holding the phone in front of you?"

"No, next to my ear so I can hear you well."

Carla chuckled. "Cathy, this is supposed to be a face-to-face chat.

Turn on your speaker and hold the phone in front of your face. Then we can see each other as we talk."

Cathy did what Carla suggested and then giggled. She'd thought they had to take turns looking at each other for a second or two and then return their phones to their ears in order to converse. *Ah, technology!* Cathy sighed. She had a lot to learn, but it was going to be fun.

TECH TIP

You'll enjoy the apps on your smartphone if you learn to use them.

Reflection

My God turns my darkness into light (Psalm 18:28).

Contemplation

"Never fight an inanimate object."

P.J. O'Rourke

Timely Prayer

Lord, this age thing is catching up with me. I have to read instructions in order to use a telephone. Imagine that.

53

Lights, Camera, Action!

Millie loved her new iPhone. She could do things with it that defied her imagination, such as sending text messages to her children and grand-kids, enjoying FaceChat, Facebook, and Twitter. What fun! She was excited about using the camera too, especially on her upcoming trip to Italy to visit her brother and his family.

"I decided to practice taking photos so I wouldn't mess up on my vacation," she said. Millie handed the iPhone to her son for some instructions when her four-year-old grandson, Conner, grabbed it from his dad's hands.

"Let me do it, Dad! I'm great at taking pictures."

"Since when?" his dad asked and chuckled. Millie stood in awe that the little boy even knew what they were talking about. Conner clicked on the camera app and started taking photos of everyone in the room, one after another, as fast as he could.

"I couldn't believe he knew what he was doing. I thought it was a fluke. But no, he was right on target."

"See, Grandma? It's a snap. Old people can do it too. Want to try?"

Millie ruffled Conner's hair. "You little dickens. You've passed me up, and you're only four years old. Yes, please show Grandma how you did that."

When Millie returned from her trip overseas, she and Conner put together a slideshow of photos to post on the Internet. Conner knew how to do that too.

TECH TIP

When you're stuck, call in the grandkid brigade. They know more about smartphones and the Internet than some professionals.

Reflection

You have been my hope, Sovereign LORD (Psalm 71:5).

Contemplation

"If you do not change direction, you may end up where you are headed."

LAO TZU

Timely Prayer

Lord, every day I consider your many gifts. I praise you for helping me out of the jams I get myself into.

54

Cellitis

Hal purchased cell phones for his elderly parents. They'd been relying on their old rotary-dial style from the 1970s for too long. He wanted to escort them into the twenty-first century despite their resistance.

"Why spend your money on this newfangled phone when ours works perfectly? Save your cash," said his dad.

His mother chimed in, "I don't see how a phone can work if it's not plugged in."

"Trust me," said Hal. "It can. I want the two of you to be safe when you're at home and away from home. This way you'll each have a phone right with you at all times—when you're shopping, at church, even working in the yard. What do you say?"

The couple agreed with some reluctance. "All right," said Hal's dad finally. "If it'll make you happy."

Hal's mom looked at her husband and sighed. Then she said, "Let's give it a try."

Hal spent some time showing his parents how to use the phones. He even bought the kind with large numbers so they could punch in the correct phone numbers without straining their eyes. He also put his cell phone number on auto-dial for them. All his parents had to do was touch one number and they could reach him immediately.

After several months, Hal's parents were avid users. They called their son often, and when he didn't answer, they'd leave a message. But whenever Hal called them, neither one of them answered their phone. Finally, Hal asked them about this odd situation. "You two must be on the move a lot more than usual," he said. "Every time I call you, I get your voice mail."

Hal's mom smiled and winked. "Your father doesn't want to run down the battery," she said, "so we shut off the phone after we call you. We want you to know we're just fine."

"But, Mom, sometimes it would be nice to have a conversation, you know? If you leave me a message, I'll call back and then we can talk."

"But what about the battery? If it goes dead, we'll be in big trouble. Who do we call? I doubt Triple-A replaces phone batteries—or do they?" she asked with a twinkle in her eye.

"Mom, remember the cord I left on your kitchen counter? As I told you, just plug one end into the phone and the other into a socket on the wall. If you do that each night before you go to bed and then unplug it in the morning, your battery will stay charged all day and charge at night. Then you can make calls and receive them anytime."

Hal's mom and dad looked at each other in surprise. "Now there's a great idea!" his dad said.

TECH TIP

Charge your phone battery once a day, and you'll always stay connected.

Reflection

Cast your cares on the Lord and
he will sustain you (Psalm 55:22).

Contemplation

"Technology is anything that wasn't around
when you were born."

Alan Kay

Timely Prayer

Lord, I like having a phone to connect with my kids, but to be honest, I'd prefer a visit.

Social Media
Meddlings

55

"Friending" the Friendless

Sharon talked her mom, Pat, into getting a Facebook account. It took a bit of doing, but finally her mother agreed. "After I explained how much fun it would be to keep up with her grandchildren and friends across the country without having to write letters, she caught on and let me help her get set up. We chose a photo for her profile, and she filled in her personal info."

Sharon also showed her mom how to check each day for new messages. Pat got the hang of it fairly quickly and enjoyed the photos and comments from other people, especially her grandkids. In fact, she even learned how to change her profile picture when she wanted to and post a few photos of her own.

"She felt quite proud of herself," Sharon said, "for doing these things without my help."

After several weeks of visiting Facebook each morning, Pat called Sharon one day in exasperation.

"Mom, you sound terrible. What's going on?" Sharon was instantly worried that her mother was ill or had fallen and needed help. But no such thing had occurred.

"I'm going off Facebook!" Pat said. "I'm disgusted with the process. I'm being bombarded by requests from people who are so desperate for friends they want to be friends with me. I'm in my eighties! I have enough friends to last me the rest of my life, and I can't even keep up with all of them. If Facebook is a place for the friendless, then it's not for me. I don't want to hurt anyone's feelings, but this is too much,

Sharon. I can't make friends with all these strangers. My life is too busy to take on more."

Pat hesitated. Then, in a quiet voice, she asked Sharon what to do. "How do I tell these poor souls that I have enough friends, and I don't have room in my life for any more?"

"Mom, I see your point." Sharon chuckled. "Let's talk about this when I visit next week. Meanwhile, hold on. I think we can fix this without you having to quit Facebook or insult anyone."

TECH TIP

Facebook friends are simply people who want to get to know you in a casual way, view your photos and comments, and share theirs with you. It's safe and fun and requires only the amount of time *you* wish to give them—from a few moments to several hours.

Reflection

Be strong and courageous (Deuteronomy 31:6).

Contemplation

"To err is human, but to really foul things up
you need a computer."
PAUL R. EHRLICH

Timely Prayer

Dear God, some of these social-media opportunities seem confusing. I feel like backing away. But if I'm to keep participating in life, I need to learn, and to grow, and to make choices based on knowledge instead of fear.

56

Something New

Henry signed up for Facebook. Most of his friends ignored social media, but Henry wasn't like them. He wanted to post pictures and bits of news from his world and find out what was going on in the lives of others, especially now that he was older and no longer drove a car. He enjoyed jumping on the Internet each day and checking in to Facebook. He shared a line or two about what he was up to that day and posted photos of friends or family members. Then he sat back and waited for the comments to come in. It was so enjoyable to read what other people had to say.

His granddaughter taught him how to take a photo of himself with his smartphone and then post it to Facebook. So he often did that. Or he asked a friend to do it for him as he posed in one funny way or another to attract attention.

One day he turned the camera on himself and snapped it, and then sent it over Facebook with this comment: "Here I am with my new goat. But don't let this picture get your goat. Ha ha!"

Comments came in...

"I see you, but where's your goat?"

"Where's he hiding?"

"What his name?"

Huh? Henry thought they were all nuts. He looked at the photo again. Wasn't it obvious what he was referring to? Why, his new goatee, of course. But when he reviewed what he'd written it was clearly his mistake. He'd typed the word *goat* instead of *goatee*!

TECH TIP

Take an extra moment or two to review what you wrote before posting or you may have some explaining to do to your Facebook friends.

Reflection

[The LORD says,] "I will rejoice in doing them good" (Jeremiah 32:41).

Contemplation

"It's fine to have social media that connects us with old friends, but we need tools that help us discover new people as well."

ETHAN ZUCKERMAN

Timely Prayer

Lord, I'm never really alone or lonely with you, my family, and my dearest friends in my life.

57

Net [Not] Working

Jason works for a company that supports connections and email for Internet Service Providers. Some of the older customers don't understand the limitations of his work. One Monday morning, a customer named Mike called in. "I signed up with your company so I could reach the entire Internet, not just some itty-bitty part of it."

"I understand you're annoyed, and you'd like me to fix the problem. Correct?"

"Well, yes."

"All right then. What are you trying to reach online?"

"I want to find a certain woman, but it says I'm not signed up."

"What do you mean by 'it'?"

"The website. I know my friend belongs to LinkedIn, but I can't find her there."

"Are you a member of LinkedIn? If not, you can't contact her. There are privacy..."

"What's so private about wanting to send someone a simple message?" Mike cut in.

"You can send her a message if she gives you her contact information, but otherwise you can't. This is pretty much true throughout the Internet. Most social network users want to protect their privacy. As I started to say, if you want to sign up for Facebook or LinkedIn or any other social network, that is up to you. Your Internet Service Provider doesn't make decisions like that for you."

Mike raised his voice. "That's ridiculous! I paid for complete access to the Internet, and that's what I expect! Now what are you going to do about it?"

Jason decided to calm the guy down by walking him through the process of signing up for LinkedIn, knowing it wasn't part of his job. It took about fifteen minutes because Mike seemed unable to take directions without repeatedly questioning everything.

"Okay, Mike," Jason said, "you're all signed up. Go make some friends! I hope you find the woman you've been looking for."

Mike exploded. "You're kidding! You mean there's more to this process? I'm done. *You* make some friends for me. That's what I'm paying you for."

Jason breathed deep. "Sorry, Mike. You must take it from here. I've done all I can."

TECH TIP

Social networking groups such as Facebook, Twitter, and LinkedIn are available to anyone who wishes to sign up, but you have to do so. Google how to get started.

Reflection

You need to persevere (Hebrews 10:36).

Contemplation

"You can't just ask customers what they want and then try to give that to them. By the time you get it built, they'll want something new."

STEVE JOBS

Timely Prayer

Lord, give me patience and kindness with those who want to help me sort out this tech stuff. Help me be willing to learn rather than blame someone.

58

Fierce Competition

Wilson took the bait—he admits—and switched from one promotional service and product to another at a lower price in order to generate leads for his online business. But after a month of using the new service, he was totally frustrated. When he called with a question, no one answered the phone. When he sent an email no one replied. One day he decided to ask for help from the first company he'd used. He'd always had excellent service in the past, so maybe he could receive it again. He gave them a call.

"Hi, there. I'm so glad you answered the phone. I'm desperate for some help. I have a couple of questions that I hope you can answer."

"Your name and account number, please," asked the agent.

"Wilson Gebhardt. I can't remember my account number."

"No problem. It will take just a moment for me to scan the client list. I see your name, sir, but your account was closed at your request. Are you calling to reinstate? If so, we're glad you've come back to us."

"No, no. I'm still with CountOnUs. But I'm finding the service so confusing. You people have always been so helpful so I thought I'd call you."

"You're asking me to help you figure out how to use our competitor's service?"

"Yes! I'm out of my mind with all this confusion. It will take just a minute, and then I'll get right off the phone and do whatever you tell me to do." He let out a long breath.

"I'm sorry," the agent replied, "but I can't offer support for our competitor's service or products. You'll have to call them."

"Well, their tech support is nonexistent. No one answers the phone or email. I don't understand what to do. Please?"

"I can tell you're upset, but I don't have access to their products. I can't answer your questions."

"Well, what am I paying for if you refuse to help me?"

"Nothing. You're not paying us a dime. You dropped us and switched to the other company."

"Well, now I see why I did. You're no help at all." And with that, Wilson hung up.

TECH TIP

Don't expect companies to provide tech support for other companies. Each company has its own technical team to deal with its own specific products and services.

Reflection

A heart at peace gives life to the body (Proverbs 14:30).

Contemplation

"Technology…is a queer thing. It brings you great gifts
with one hand, and it stabs you in the back with the other."

CARRIE SNOW

Timely Prayer

God, too often I'm ready to blame someone else for my own mistakes. Please give me the gifts of discernment, humility, and patience.

59

Facing Facebook

Alice called her daughter Sue for some help getting on Facebook. Many of her friends were posting comments and photos, and Alice didn't want to be left out. But for the life of her, she couldn't get the hang of it.

Sue told her to start by typing into her Internet browser www .Facebook.com.

"What's a browser?" Alice asked.

"It's the program you use to get on the Internet, Mom. You know, 'Safari' or 'Firefox.' I forget which one you use."

"I forget too. What do they look like?"

"Safari looks like a compass, and Firefox looks like a blue ball wrapped with a tongue of fire. Check and see which one you have in your applications."

"What do you mean 'in my applications'? Where are they? I don't know what you're talking about."

"Mom, I know you do. Remember when you looked up the recipe for snickerdoodles? You found it on your own. You even called me to tell me how excited you were."

"That was different. That was for a cookie recipe. This Facebook thing is totally different."

"But, Mom, you use the same browser to find everything on the Internet. A browser is a search engine. You just type in...oh never mind. Looks like this calls for an in-person visit!"

"You mean you'll come over here and help me set up Facebook?"

"Sure. When's a good time for you?"

"Anytime. Looks like I've found a way to see you more often."

"Mom…"

TECH TIP

One way to stay in close touch with your grown kids and grandkids is to open a Facebook account. Once you do, you'll love it. You may even bump into some old friends you haven't seen in years.

Reflection

The righteous choose their friends carefully (Proverbs 12:26).

Contemplation

"Do not protect yourself by a fence,
but rather by your friends."

CZECH PROVERB

Timely Prayer

Lord, thank you for the gift of friendship…and, most of all, that *you* call me friend.

Fun Quiz #4

Circle the correct answer for each question.

1. Firefox, Opera, Chrome, Safari, and Explorer are types of what?

    Internet browsers   clothing stores   computer brands

2. What company did Bill Gates found?

    National Insurance   Microsoft   Google

3. What is Nintendo?

    Japanese electronics company   video game   type of computer

4. What is the name of the flashing thingamabob on the computer screen?

    byte   cursor   pointer

5. What is the handheld device used to make selections on the computer screen called?

    mouse   stylus   brush

6. What is the part of the computer where information is displayed called?

    monitor   frame   screen

ANSWERS

1. Internet browsers; 2. Microsoft; 3. Japanese electronics company; 4. cursor;
5. mouse; 6. monitor.

149

Harebrained
Hardware

iBad

Jessica bought her father, Asim, an iPad for his birthday one year so he could take photos, read ebooks, play games, and access email. He was very pleased with the device and took to it right away.

The grandkids were proud of him. Grandpa could now interact with them wherever they were. Asim's native language was Arabic, so translations into English for his grandkids were sometimes a struggle. He did his best to keep up with the children and to learn their catch phrases.

One day Asim reported to Jessica that he'd heard the kids often say, "My bad." He didn't understand.

"It's a silly expression," she said, "and it's not good English. It means 'my mistake' or 'I'm to blame.'"

Asim shook his head but laughed it off. "Kids today. Who can tell what they are up to?"

A few days later while the grandkids were visiting, Grandpa Asim opened his iPad to show them some photos he'd taken. "Take a look at my iBad," he said.

The boy and girl chuckled. "Grandpa," Angela said, "that's an *iPad*, not an *iBad*." She emphasized each word so he could distinguish the difference in sounds.

"My bad," he chirped. The three burst out laughing.

TECH TIP

Keep up on the latest buzzwords your grandkids are using. It will help communication and, perhaps, make you smile.

Reflection

In this world you will have trouble. But take heart!
I have overcome the world (John 16:33).

Contemplation

"Technology has to be invented or adopted."

JARED DIAMOND

Timely Prayer

I can see, Lord, that I need a sense of humor if I'm going to make it through the tech maze and keep up with my grandkids.

61

All Keyed Up

Joyce and her friend Louellen met for breakfast at their favorite spot. They enjoyed catching up with one another's family news over an omelet and coffee. Afterward, they lingered in the parking lot next to Joyce's car for a few more minutes of conversation. Then they said goodbye.

Joyce took out her remote and clicked the button, but nothing happened. She pressed the open button several more times, but her car remained locked. How frustrating! She had things to do and places to go. This was no time for the remote to act up.

She rushed over to her friend's car just as Louellen was about to pull away. Joyce tapped on the driver's-side window. "I'm stuck," she said after Louellen slid the window open. "This blasted remote chose today to misbehave. I might need a ride home. Can you hold on a minute while I try again?"

"No problem."

Joyce ran back to her car. She suddenly thought of what to do. She hit the lock button and then the open button. The car unlocked. What a relief. She waved to Louellen, and then slid into the car seat and drove home. Wouldn't her husband, Miles, be proud of her when she told him her quick thinking?

He turned to her with a puzzled expression on his face when she finished reciting her dilemma and the solution. "Why didn't you just use the key in the door?"

Oh my! Joyce was sure her face was turning red. *Now that's what comes from doing things one way for so long that the obvious escaped me.*

TECH TIP

Always have a backup plan in case the one you rely on fails.

Reflection

God is not a God of disorder
but of peace (1 Corinthians 14:33).

Contemplation

"Technology is supposed to make our lives easier…
But too often it seems to make things harder."

James Surowiecki

Timely Prayer

Lord, it's such good news that I don't need a remote control to catch your attention.

62

All Gone

"Reg, can you help me out? I'm just finishing my shift, and a man came in for a task that's going to take a little time."

Reg agreed. His partner, Donny, nodded his thanks, grabbed his jacket, and walked out of the tech-support room.

The customer explained that he wanted to have his hard drive deleted because he planned to purchase a new computer and give this one to his granddaughter, who was starting high school and needed a laptop.

Reg explained what he planned to do, just in case the man had any questions. "I'm going to go into your computer and delete all your files on your hard drive. Is that what you want? You understand this will delete everything you have except actual programs?"

"Yep. I'm just glad you can do it for me. I was afraid to tackle this on my own."

Reg gave the customer one more chance. "Okay, I will delete *everything personal* you have on your hard drive so the computer will be clean for your granddaughter. You have all of your important documents backed up, correct? So you can transfer them to your new computer?"

"Yes! What are you waiting for? Go ahead and delete."

"Okay." Reg started the delete process. Then realizing the man had about three gigs of data, he stopped and said again, "You have quite a bit of data here. I want to make sure you backed up everything you need because once I complete this, it will all be gone."

"All good. Go for it."

"Okay."

After the deleting process was finished, the customer piped up. "The files that were on my desktop—now where are they hiding? Can you tell me how to transfer them to my new computer?"

Reg stared at the customer and then took two deep breaths. "The files on your desktop? Remember, you told me you backed up everything and to go ahead and delete all your personal information. That included what was on the desktop."

The customer let out a nervous laugh. "I hate to admit it, but I'm not too savvy with computers. What does 'backup' mean, actually?"

TECH TIP

Better to be sure you understand what you're asking someone to do than to be sorry later because you didn't ask or get all the details.

Reflection

Call on me in the day of trouble (Psalm 50:15).

Contemplation

"Never trust anything that can think for itself if you can't see where it keeps its brain."

J.K. ROWLING

Timely Prayer

God, sometimes I let pride get in the way of common sense, and then I pay the price. Thank you for standing with me and helping me find a way out.

63

Fan Club

Randy phoned his tech-savvy grandson Greg. "I have a huge problem," he bellowed into the phone.

"You sound breathless, Grandpa. What's going on?" Greg frowned, worrying that his grandfather had been in some kind of accident or something.

"My computer fan jammed. It's stopped working completely." Randy let out a deep breath. "If it's not one thing, it's another."

"I'll come right over," said Greg. "I think it's about time you got rid of that dinosaur and bought a new laptop. I'll help you pick out the perfect one for you. What do you say?"

"Not if you can fix the fan. I hate wasting my retirement money, you know that."

"But, Grandpa," said Greg, "you enjoy playing on the computer. It's one of your pleasures at this time of your life. Why not spend some of that money on yourself? After all, you earned it."

"We'll talk about that later. Just come on over and see what you can do to unjam the fan."

Greg hustled over. When he took a look at the computer, he saw that it was working and the fan was running, although it was making more noise than usual. "No worries, Grandpa. The fan isn't jammed. It probably just needs a good cleaning."

"How do you know? Don't you have to open up the computer to look?"

"Nope. If the fan had really stopped working, your computer would be on fire."

"Oh!" Randy scratched his head. "I think I'll take you up on your idea. Let's shop for a new computer and let this one rest in peace."

"Good idea!" Greg clapped his grandfather on the shoulder, and the two headed out to the computer store.

TECH TIP

There are times when it's not worth being penny-wise and pound-foolish. When it comes to technology, play it safe and stay up-to-date.

Reflection

[Jesus said,] "Your Father knows what you need before you ask him" (Matthew 6:8).

Contemplation

"If we continue to develop our technology without wisdom or prudence, our servant may prove to be our executioner."

OMAR BRADLEY

Timely Prayer

Lord, please help me accept the things I can't change and change what I can that needs it.

64

Run for Cover

Liz ran into her neighbor Mitch in front of the community mailboxes.

"So Liz," he said, "what's up with you these days? Haven't seen you in a while. How's that new computer working for you? I thought it was pretty brave of you to take that on at your age."

Liz didn't know whether to smile or sass Mitch. What did he know about computers? He was an old dinosaur who refused to join the twenty-first century. At least she was willing to try to stay current.

"It's fine. Really, I'm loving it—though I must admit I'm having a bit of a struggle getting used to the mouse. It's tricky. Sometimes it works and sometimes it doesn't. Can't figure out how to handle that. Guess I'll have to call the tech support number and find out."

"Maybe I can help," said Mitch. "I'll take a look. It could be an easy solution."

Liz felt her face flush. "What do you know about computers?" she barked. "You don't even have one."

"But I know what a mouse is. Everyone who has a computer has a mouse. I've watched my grands whenever I visit them."

Liz threw up her hands. "Can't hurt. Maybe we'll figure it out together. I'll buy you a coffee if you can make it work."

Liz invited Mitch in, and the pair looked at the mouse.

Mitch burst out laughing.

Liz frowned. "What's so funny?"

He picked up the mouse and pointed to the cover. "It's the plastic packaging that's causing the problem. Take out the mouse, toss the plastic, and you'll be in business."

Liz could barely look at her neighbor. He'd caught on faster than she had. How embarrassing.

"Now about that coffee. When's a good day for you?" Mitch asked.

TECH TIP

Before you reach for the phone to call tech support, take a moment to use some common sense. You might be surprised at how that will help you solve your problem.

Reflection

Grace to all who love our Lord Jesus Christ (Ephesians 6:24).

Contemplation

"Without a struggle there can be no progress."
FREDERICK DOUGLASS

Timely Prayer

Lord, I notice my impatience to reach my goal—whether large or small. Help me to accept challenges as part of the process.

65

Kick the Kindle

Lorna's Auntie Jane enjoyed her weekly walk to the local library. She was a reader, and it was a pleasure to pick out three books each Monday afternoon. Sometimes her aunt read even more in a week. She enjoyed telling anyone who'd listen all the titles of books she'd read; she kept a list pinned to her kitchen bulletin board.

Lorna often joined Jane, and the two would stop for tea and a blueberry muffin at a teashop in town. Auntie Jane was a creature of habit. Lorna admired the woman, but she also felt that her aunt was losing touch with the times. Perhaps she would enjoy life more if she took advantage of some technology, such as a computer or e-reader.

In early December one year, Lorna decided to surprise Auntie Jane with a Kindle as a Christmas gift. She was tickled with the idea. Now her aunt could download hundreds of titles to one machine and not have to lug books home from the library each week. Lorna purchased the e-reader, wrapped it in lovely gift paper, and put a bright-red ribbon on top. She knew it might take a little getting used to, but she felt certain her aunt would love this new and convenient way to keep all her favorite books in one lightweight device.

On Christmas Eve, Lorna stopped by Auntie Jane's house to drop off the gift.

"Come right in, dear! Merry Christmas!" Jane said as she invited Lorna in for tea. The two chatted a bit before Lorna handed Jane the gift.

Auntie Jane opened the box and her eyes lit up. "This looks so special. What is it?"

Lorna explained that it was an e-reader and how she could download books from a digital book company, such as amazon.com. The device could hold hundreds of books. She'd be able to read books without the bother of a library card, a deadline for returning the book, and the weight of carrying volumes back and forth. She wouldn't have to go out in the rain anymore. Lorna assured her aunt that she would help her get started.

Auntie Jane looked at Lorna and smiled. "Thank you, dear, for thinking of me, but I couldn't possibly accept this very kind and thoughtful gift. I know I won't use it. You see I *like* to walk to the library. I love the smell of the place. I enjoy the beauty and order of shelves of books. I like sitting in an easy chair and turning the pages of the magazines and daily newspaper. I know a lot of people are excited about these new-fangled inventions, but I'm an old-fangled woman who likes things just the way they are."

Lorna smiled and understood even as she realized she'd misread her aunt by a mile.

TECH TIP

Some people love the idea of carrying books with them on a small device. If you're one of them, ask for help getting started.

Reflection

What you decide on will be done (Job 22:28).

Contemplation

"Never trust anyone who has not brought a book with them."

LEMONY SNICKET
(DANIEL HANDLER)

Timely Prayer

Lord, the best book of all is the Bible. Thank you that your Word leads me in all the best ways.

66

Decisions...Decisions!

Maureen was quite pleased with herself. She'd just turned seventy and wanted to stay in touch with the times. No more making excuses for not learning to use a computer and for falling behind in state-of-the-art communication. Many of her friends hid behind their fears. They worried they might not be sharp enough to work a computer or that getting and maintaining one was too expensive for their Social Security-based budgets. But most of them, in Maureen's opinion, were simply scaredy-cats. But not her.

She drove to the local computer store and asked for a consultation with one of the salespeople.

Sergio walked over, introduced himself, and shook her hand. He suggested they sit down and talk about what might be the best buy for her. "I'd like to ask you a few questions," he said. "For example, how will you use a computer? Do you want to create documents, such as letters or spreadsheets for finances? Or will you prefer to stick to email only? Maybe you'd like to get into social media—you know, Facebook, Pinterest, or Twitter?"

The young man was all smiles and very encouraging. He didn't talk down to her, and he didn't assume what she knew or didn't know. On the other hand, she felt as though he were talking over her head. She'd heard the word "twitter," of course, but the name in this context sounded odd to her. She'd always associated the word with birds.

Maureen didn't want to sound like an old lady who didn't have a clue as to what was going on in the world. She was eager to get with the program, so to speak, and answer intelligently, as well as ask questions of her own. She paused for a moment, adjusted herself in the chair, and looked Sergio in the eye. "Before we get to the particulars," she asked, "which do you recommend—hardware or software?"

TECH TIP

Hardware is the computer itself. Software is the name for the programs and operation information the computer uses to take in and process information.

Reflection

Let the wise listen and add to their learning,
and let the discerning get guidance (Proverbs 1:5).

Contemplation

"Risk comes from not knowing what you're doing."
WARREN BUFFETT

Timely Prayer

Lord, I don't like looking foolish, but, on the other hand, that's what it takes sometimes to get where I want to go.

67

Frozen Tundra

Paul walked into the den and turned on his computer, but nothing happened. No sound, no images on the screen, nothing at all. He slapped the desk in frustration. "This is one too many times this computer has let me down. Time for a new machine!"

"I heard that!" his wife, Sally, called from the hallway. "We are not going through this again. Every time something goes wrong with the computer, or the washer, or the dryer, or the TV, you're ready to dole out thousands of dollars to replace it. But not this time. I put my foot down. Do you hear me? We live on a budget."

"Yes, I hear you. But you don't understand. Playing games and sending email and trading jokes is about all I have left to enjoy. I need my computer to operate properly. It's old and it's cranky."

"Sounds like someone I know," Sally muttered.

"Okay, I won't buy a new one. But I'll need someone to help me out of this jam."

Sally snapped, "Call tech support. That's what you need—support—not another computer to mess with."

Paul placed the call and listened as the rep asked a few questions and then concluded, "It sounds to me like your system has frozen. I'll send someone out. The first available day we have is Friday at..."

"I don't know why you think it's frozen. I just checked the thermostat, and it's almost 80 degrees in here. I'm sweltering."

TECH TIP

When a computer "freezes," it has nothing to do with the weather. It means the system has locked up. You may need to shut down and start again or take it in for repair.

Reflection

Anxiety weighs down the heart, but a kind word cheers it up (Proverbs 12:25).

Contemplation

"Being at ease with not knowing is crucial for answers to come to you."

ECKHART TOLLE

Timely Prayer

Thank you, God, for always providing the wisdom I need when I need it.

Password Paranoia

68

One Key at a Time

Harvey had quite a challenge on his hands helping his brother Hector learn to use a computer. Teaching Hector to log on so he could proceed with what he wanted to do became a repeated and major event.

"I told him to type in his first name and the year of his birth." Harvey knew that was simple enough that Hector wouldn't forget. "That's your username," said Harvey.

"Whatever." Hector hunched his shoulders and stared at the keyboard as though it had just dropped in from outer space. Then he put his hands over the keys and several seconds later he hit the shift key and the "h." Then he hunted for the letter "e" and so on, until he'd finished typing in his name. He was on the hunt, and it took him a full two minutes to get that far. When it came to inserting his birth year, the process started all over again.

"When was I born?" he asked.

"Hector, you're kidding me! You don't remember the year you were born?"

"No. If I did, I wouldn't be asking."

Harvey threw up his hands and leaned over. He wasn't about to wait another two minutes while his brother hunted for the keys. He typed in 1927 and then stepped back.

Next came choosing a password. Harvey let out a long wheeze. "What's your favorite fruit?" he asked. "We'll make that word your password so you can get into the computer each day."

"Banana."

"Perfect. Not too long and also easy to remember."

Hector found the "b" key right away, but he had a hard time locating the "a." "Shouldn't the 'a' be next to the 'b'?" he asked.

"The keyboard doesn't work that way," said Harvey. "Here, I'll give you some help." He typed in the "a" and followed it with the "n." So far so good. "Now all you have to do is type the rest 'a-n-a.'"

"I don't see an 'ana' on this keyboard," Hector said with a straight face. "All my keys have one letter each."

Harvey caught his breath, deciding in that moment that he'd better get out of his brother's house before frustration overtook him.

TECH TIP

Before getting started on a computer, it's best to take a class for beginners.

Reflection

The heart of the discerning acquires knowledge (Proverbs 18:15).

Contemplation

"Life is a series of experiences, each one of which makes us bigger, even though sometimes it is hard to realize this."

HENRY FORD

Timely Prayer

Lord, thank you for your patience with me and for the patience you give me as I learn.

69

Star-Studded Password

"Brent, I'm so frustrated I could take this keyboard and toss it out the window!"

"Settle down, Mom. It's probably something simple. Tell me what's going on, and I'll help you out." Brent walked over to his mother, who was sitting stiffly at the kitchen table while drumming against the keyboard on her laptop as if it was a piano with sticky keys.

"The thing just doesn't work." She let out a sigh. "Watch this. I'm trying to create an account at Melissa's Favorite Recipes, but it's not working even though I've gone over the instructions again and again. How hard can it be?"

"I agree." Brent urged his mom to relax, take a breath, and take him through the process slowly.

"When I type the password I selected, none of the letters show up. No matter how many times I've tried, all I get is a little row of stars— you know, those asterisk thingies. I'm not even touching that key, but it still appears on the screen."

Brent leaned down and kissed his mom on the cheek. "It's okay, really. In fact, you are doing just what you're supposed to do. Nothing is wrong."

"That's ridiculous. How does the person at the other end know if I'm sending the right password or not if all you can see is a bunch of little stars?"

"It's for security, Mom, so no one can steal your password and break into your account."

"Well, now I've heard everything! I'm sure Bill Gates has more to do than try to steal my password."

"You're right about that, Mom. But trust me. This is the only way you're going to be able to create an account with Melissa's Favorite Recipes. Shall we proceed or not?"

"Proceed. But it was much easier in the old days. I could just buy a cookbook at the store and be done with it."

TECH TIP

Some of the tech rules may not make sense to you, but follow them anyway. You'll get to where you want to go that way.

Reflection

The Lord will give you insight (2 Timothy 2:7).

Contemplation

"Confusion makes people uncomfortable.
They can't put their finger on it."
LENNY KRAVITZ

Timely Prayer

Lord God, thank you that you check me when I get overwrought. Help me turn to you first, not last.

70

I Pass

Irma walked into the computer store and knew right away she was out of her element. Tall, gangly salespeople roamed the aisles. One young man came straight toward her.

"Good afternoon, ma'am. My name is Ben. Are you looking for something in particular?"

"Not exactly," she said. "I think I have the equipment I need, but I don't know how to use it. I mean I'd like to send an email to my grandson, and I can't seem to get the hang of it."

"I can help you with that. We have a demo model over here. Let's take a look."

Irma followed Ben to the next aisle. The young man opened an email tutorial and began walking her through the steps to send an email. He indicated the "To" and "From" boxes and pointed to the example: "To: Sam64@city.com."

"That won't work," she said, feeling agitated. "My grandson's name is Peter, and there are no numbers in his email address. It's PeterPenny@aol.com."

"I understand, ma'am. This is just an example to illustrate what to do."

"I won't know what to do if you don't use the correct information. And besides that I don't think I bought the right computer because I don't see a key for aol.com. I don't see it on your computer either. Now what am I going to do? This is all just too complicated." Irma hooked her purse over her shoulder and stuck out her hand to Ben. "Thanks for trying to help me. I think I'll write him a letter instead."

TECH TIP

Don't give up too soon. You can do whatever is required—if you really want to.

Reflection

If you believe, you will receive whatever you ask for in prayer (Matthew 21:22).

Contemplation

"The most certain way to succeed is always to try just one more time."
THOMAS A. EDISON

Timely Prayer

Thank you, Lord, for reminding me in your Word that you are a God of order not confusion and that you will help me solve any problem I have.

71

Pick a Password

Rosie strode up the walkway to her neighbor's house. Ron was a genius when it came to all things computer related. Everyone in their senior community agreed. He made a little pocket money helping anyone who needed it, and today it was Rosie's turn. She'd heard how important it is to change passwords every couple of months, especially for her bank or investment company, because a thief could steal her funds with a few clicks of a mouse.

"To be sure you're safe," Ron suggested, "your new passwords should contain a combination of numbers, upper- and lowercase letters of the alphabet, and a couple of punctuation symbols—you know like an asterisk or an exclamation point."

"Really? Sounds complicated," Rosie said. "I'm just your average citizen, not some espionage agent that has millions of dollars and government secrets to protect. Can't I simplify the process?"

"All the more reason to be safe," he said. "The sly ones target us oldsters. We need to outsmart them with complex passwords."

"All right, I'll try. But I don't know what you mean by upper- and lowercase letters. Start there, please."

"When we were kids we used to call them big letters and small letters or capital letters and little ones."

"Well, why didn't you say that to start with? You don't need to be pretentious with me. We've been friends for years. Keep your technical language for someone else."

TECH TIP

It's worth learning the ropes of the tech world—even if you're getting up there in years.

Reflection

*Make every effort to add to your faith goodness;
and to goodness, knowledge* (2 Peter 1:5).

Contemplation

"Tell me and I forget. Teach me and I remember.
Involve me and I learn."
BENJAMIN FRANKLIN

Timely Prayer

Lord, how grateful I am that when I study your Word I learn what really matters. Open my mind to the wisdom you have for me in all areas of my life.

Tech Support
Troubles

72

Pretty Cool

Grandpa strode into his grandson's room. "What're you doing, Ricky?"

"Nothin' much. Just playing on the computer and lookin' up some songs to download. How about you, Grandpa?"

"I'm killing some time while I wait for my modem to calm down."

"Calm down?" Ricky looked at his grandfather and frowned. "What do you mean? Is it hyperactive?" Then he broke into a belly laugh.

"Something like that. It won't connect. Being temperamental."

"Maybe I can help. Is it still hooked up?" Ricky sounded sure it would be an easy fix. "I'll take a look."

"No, I pulled the cord."

"Well, we can't find out the problem if it's not hooked up. Where is it?"

"Where it belongs—the fridge."

"What?" Ricky jumped up. "Why there? Are you planning to serve it for dinner?"

Grandpa frowned.

"It's a joke," Rick admitted. "I just never heard of putting a modem in the refrigerator. Why there?"

"I noticed it got really hot, and I wanted to cool it down. I considered the freezer for a faster cool-off, but I thought the freezer might damage it."

"Grandpa, it looks like we'll be making a trip to the computer store. Fridge or freezer, I'm guessing you're going to need a new modem."

TECH TIP

Avoid diagnosing tech problems yourself if you don't have the expertise. Let the "tech doctor" run the exam.

Reflection

We all stumble in many ways (James 3:2).

Contemplation

"It's always helpful to learn from your mistakes because then your mistakes seem worthwhile."

GARRY MARSHALL

Timely Prayer

Dear God, I'm embarrassed when I mess up, but maybe it's good that I do because then I realize I'm a human being and only you can set me straight.

73

Got It Covered

Arny answered a request from his boss to take a service call at the Midtown Senior Services Center. The staff needed a professional to come in to install and update everyone's software and to provide a short tutoring session so each person would be clear about the newest changes. He knew he was in for some strange questions, and that he'd have to speak slowly and avoid computereze when possible. These folks were over the hill, he surmised, and weren't likely to be interested in the technology behind the software. They just wanted to get their computers up and running so they could respond to emails, keep lists, compose forms and letters, and do anything else related to running a community service agency. He needed to show them as clearly and succinctly as possible what to do and how to do it.

The tech company Arny worked for supported Microsoft Windows, so before starting his task, Arny wanted to be certain the manager knew what he was there to do—that they were in sync. He approached the gray-haired gentleman sitting at the large desk in the middle of the room.

"Good morning, sir. I'm here from ABC Tech Support. As you probably know, we install and support MS Windows. Just want to be sure we're clear about what I can offer you today. Have you used Windows before?"

The manager stared at Arny for a moment and frowned. "This is the twenty-first century. We have air conditioning."

TECH TIP

Uh-oh! Tech blooper. There are windows in buildings and then there is Windows, a major computer operating system.

Reflection

If on some point you think differently, that too
God will make clear to you (Philippians 3:15).

Contemplation

"Maybe it's worth investigating the unknown."

Krzysztof Kieslowski

Timely Prayer

Lord, I still have so much to learn. Good thing I can ask for wisdom and you will give it to me. Thank you.

Fun Quiz #5

Put a check mark in front of the correct answer.

1. An appliance designed to protect electrical devices from voltage spikes.

   ____ surge protector

   ____ circuit breaker

2. A device that produces a paper copy of information from a computer.

   ____ scanner

   ____ printer

3. A technical term that means to change a document in some way.

   ____ crop

   ____ edit

4. What word means to erase data from a computer?

   ____ delete

   ____ scroll

5. A piece of printed information from the computer.

   ____ printout

   ____ binary code

6. Parts of a computer that you can see and physically touch.

   ____ hardware

   ____ operating system

7. The command you give when you want to keep a file on your computer.

   ____ save

   ____ store

8. When an unexpected condition occurs on the computer you may receive this.

   ____ error message

   ____ mistake made

Computer Training Resources

Note: The information for each entry was taken from the respective website. The web addresses and information may have changed.

www.seniornet.org: "SeniorNet was founded in 1986 by Dr. Mary Furlong. She realized the senior population has a great deal of talent and experience to bring to the table. Her goal was to create a sense of community for older adults where they could share what they were learning to enhance their lives and the lives of others."

www.seniorplanet.org: *"Senior Planet* is the first tech-themed resource for people over 60 who are living and aging well—with attitude."

www.skillfulsenior.com: "The perfect place for seniors to learn the skills they need. Email your grandchildren, get medical information via the Internet."

www.gcflearnfree.org/internet: "Become Internet savvy with tutorials on how to browse smartly, maintain your safety, and network socially while online."

http://www.meganga.com: "The first computer course for basic computer training is specifically aimed at seniors and beginners. Our easy-to-follow tutorials for adults start with elementary-but-essential topics, learning the computer basics before gradually moving on to more advanced computer lessons in Microsoft Office Word and Excel. Working through our free computer lessons, beginners and elderly students will gain in confidence, learn computer skills and will soon be able to do much more with their computer."

More Great Books by Karen O'Connor!

365 Senior Moments You'd Rather Forget
Gettin' Old Ain't for Wimps
Gettin' Old Ain't for Wimps! Gift Edition
God Bless My Senior Moments
The Golden Years Ain't for Wimps
Grandma, You Rock!
Lord, How Did I Get This Old So Soon?
My Favorite Senior Moments
When God Answers Your Prayers

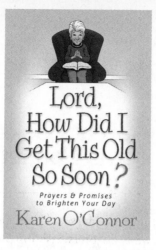

Lord, How Did I Get This Old So Soon?

Need a quick pick-me-up? Communion time with your heavenly Father? Bestselling author and gentle humorist Karen O'Connor offers sincere, real-life prayers to encourage you to open your heart and talk with God.

> *Thank you, Lord, that it's never too late to dream a new dream, repair an injured relationship, make a new friend, draw closer to you...*

> *What I need right now is a big hug, Lord. Please hold me tight and remind me that you are always here for me...*

> *My prayer is for strength today. I won't pray for a lifetime supply because I might go off on my own. I do best when I'm in touch with you daily...*

Arranged by season to reflect the time of year or how you're feeling, these heartfelt prayers highlight the grace, mercy, and blessings God provides. You'll be encouraged by these thoughts that reflect where you are, reaffirm your hope during difficult times, and reveal how much Jesus loves you.

To learn more about Harvest House books and
to read sample chapters, visit our website:

www.harvesthousepublishers.com

HARVEST HOUSE PUBLISHERS
EUGENE, OREGON